■ はしがき ■

　本書は，第一学習社発行の英語教科書「CREATIVE English Communication I」に完全準拠したワークブックです。各パート見開き 2 ページで，教科書本文を使って「聞く」「読む」「話す（やり取り）」「話す（発表）」「書く」の 4 技能 5 領域の力を育成する問題をバランスよく用意しました。

■ 本書の構成と利用法 ■

各パート，Activity Plus のページ

教科書本文

・新出単語を太字で示しました。

・意味のまとまりごとにスラッシュを入れました。ここで示した意味のまと　　　　　　　語の強弱のリズム，イントネーションなどに注意して，本文を流暢に音読できるようにしましょう。付属のスピーキング・トレーナーを使って，自分の発話を後から確認できます。発話の流暢さ（1 分あたりの発話語数：words per minute）を算出する計算式を，本書巻末にまとめて掲載しています。

📖 Reading

・大学入学共通テストなどの形式に対応した，本文の内容理解問題です。

🔎 Vocabulary & Grammar

・英検®や GTEC®の形式に対応した，新出単語や新出表現，文法事項，重要語句についての問題です。

🎧 Listening

・本文内容やテーマに関連した短い英文を聞いて答える問題です。

・Activity Plus では，本文内容やテーマに関連したやや長い英文を聞いて答える問題を収録しています。

・**CD** 💿 は別売の音声 CD のトラック番号を示します。二次元コードを読み取って，音声を PC やスマートフォンなどから聞くこともできます。

💬 Interaction

・本文内容やテーマに関連した会話を聞いて，最後の発話に対して自分の考えなどを応答し，やり取りを完成させる活動です。

・付属のスピーキング・トレーナーを使って，自分の発話を後から確認することができます。

💬 Production (Speak)　　✏️ Production (Write)

・本文内容やテーマに関連した，自分自身に関する質問や，考えや意見を問う質問に話したり書いたりして答える表現活動です。

◆「知識・技能」や「思考力・判断力・表現力」を養成することを意識し，設問ごとに主に対応する観点を示しました。

◆ライティング，スピーキング問題を自分で採点できるようにしています。

　別冊『解答・解説集』の「ルーブリック評価表」（ある観点における学習の到達度を判断する基準）を用いて，自分の記述内容や発話内容が採点できます。

CONTENTS

CAN-DO List
知識・技能

思考力・判断力・表現力

- ☐📖夢の実現に関する大谷翔平選手のメッセージについて的確に理解し，その内容を整理することができる。
- ☐🎧失敗やスポーツに関する英文を聞いて，必要な情報を把握することができる。
- ☐💬日常生活について，適切に情報や考えを伝え合うことができる。
- ☐😀スポーツについて，自分の考えを話して伝えることができる。
- ☐✍日常生活や目標について，自分の考えを書いて伝えることができる。

- ☐📖日本および世界の「弁当文化」について的確に理解し，その内容を整理することができる。
- ☐🎧食事や弁当に関する英文を聞いて，必要な情報を把握することができる。
- ☐💬弁当について，適切に情報や考えを伝え合うことができる。
- ☐😀弁当について，自分の考えを話して伝えることができる。
- ☐✍弁当について，情報や考えを書いて伝えることができる。

- ☐📖携帯電話の発展について的確に理解し，その内容を整理することができる。
- ☐🎧携帯電話に関する英文を聞いて，必要な情報を把握することができる。
- ☐💬携帯電話やアプリについて，適切に情報や考えを伝え合うことができる。
- ☐😀公衆電話について，自分の考えを話して伝えることができる。
- ☐✍携帯電話について，情報や考えを書いて伝えることができる。

- ☐📖絶滅危惧種の保護のあり方について的確に理解し，その内容を整理することができる。
- ☐🎧絶滅危惧種や寄付に関する英文を聞いて，必要な情報を把握することができる。
- ☐💬生き物や寄付について，適切に情報や考えを伝え合うことができる。
- ☐😀パンダについて，自分の考えを話して伝えることができる。
- ☐✍環境問題や寄付について，情報や考えを書いて伝えることができる。

- ☐📖『おさるのジョージ』の作者の人生について的確に理解し，その内容を整理することができる。
- ☐🎧物語や戦争，結婚，旅行に関する英文を聞いて，必要な情報を把握することができる。
- ☐💬情報収集や旅行，避難，読書について，適切に情報や考えを伝え合うことができる。
- ☐😀自分の思い出について，情報を話して伝えることができる。
- ☐✍結婚や物語登場人物の心情について，自分の考えを書いて伝えることができる。

- ☐📖ホセ・ムヒカの幸福に関するメッセージについて的確に理解し，その内容を整理することができる。
- ☐🎧服装や選挙，スピーチ，教育，幸福に関する英文を聞いて，必要な情報を把握することができる。
- ☐💬日常生活やスピーチについて，適切に情報や考えを伝え合うことができる。
- ☐😀社会問題について，自分の考えを話して伝えることができる。
- ☐✍幸福や大切なことについて，自分の考えを書いて伝えることができる。

- ☐📖海洋プラスチック汚染について的確に理解し，その内容を整理することができる。
- ☐🎧日常生活や環境に関する英文を聞いて，必要な情報を把握することができる。
- ☐💬日常生活や環境について，適切に情報や考えを伝え合うことができる。
- ☐😀SNS について，自分の考えを話して伝えることができる。
- ☐✍プラスチックについて，情報や考えを書いて伝えることができる。

- ☐📖近藤紘子さんのストーリーについて的確に理解し，その内容を整理することができる。
- ☐🎧日常生活や平和に関する英文を聞いて，必要な情報を把握することができる。
- ☐💬スピーチや平和，後悔について適切に情報や考えを伝え合うことができる。
- ☐😀怒りのコントロールについて，自分の考えを話して伝えることができる。
- ☐✍原爆や喪失感について，自分の考えを書いて伝えることができる。

- ☐📖将来の人間と AI のあるべき姿について的確に理解し，その内容を整理することができる。
- ☐🎧日常生活や AI に関する英文を聞いて，必要な情報を把握することができる。
- ☐💬日常生活や AI について，適切に情報や考えを伝え合うことができる。
- ☐😀キャッシュレス決済について，自分の考えを話して伝えることができる。
- ☐✍AI について，自分の考えを書いて伝えることができる。

- ☐📖ストーリーの展開を的確に理解し，その内容を整理することができる。
- ☐✍日常生活や物語登場人物の心情について，自分の考えを書いて伝えることができる。

You found some information / about Shohei Otani / on the Internet. // You are learning / about him. //

Shohei Otani //

Throws / Right //   Bats / Left //

Height / 193 centimeters //   **Weight** / 95 kilograms //

Date of Birth / July 5, 1994 //   Hometown / Oshu, Iwate **Prefecture** //

Motto / "Keep trying harder. // Don't be afraid / of **failure**." //

Personal History /

　　Shohei Otani began playing baseball / when he was an elementary school student. // In his high school days, / he played / in the high school baseball championships / at Koshien / twice. // In both tournaments, / his team lost / in the first game. // After he graduated / from high school, / he joined the Hokkaido Nippon-Ham Fighters. // In 2018, / he made his Major **League debut**. // He is very famous / for being good / at both **pitching** / and batting. // People / in Japan / and the U.S. / call him a "**two-way** player." // (129 words)

🔊 音読しよう

スピーキング・トレーナー

Practice 1　スラッシュ位置で文を区切って読んでみよう ☐
Practice 2　英語の強弱のリズムに注意して読んでみよう ☐
TRY!　　　　１分20秒以内に本文全体を音読しよう ☐

📖 **Reading**　本文の内容を読んで理解しよう【知識・技能】【思考力・判断力・表現力】　　共通テスト

Make the correct choice to complete each sentence or answer each question. (各4点)

1. When he was an elementary school student, Shohei Otani ☐ .

　① joined a baseball team

　② moved to Hokkaido with his family

　③ was already famous for both pitching and batting

　④ wasn't good at playing baseball

2. Which of the following is Shohei Otani's motto? ☐

　① Don't be afraid of challenging yourself.　② Don't be afraid of making mistakes.

　③ Keep being successful.　　　　　　　　　④ Keep making mistakes.

3. What are **not** known about Shohei Otani from the website? (Choose two options. The order does not matter.) ☐ · ☐

　① His age of starting baseball.

　② His birthday.

　③ The results of his team at the Koshien tournaments.

　④ The year of his first win as a professional baseball player.

🔍 Vocabulary & Grammar　　重要表現や文法事項について理解しよう【知識】　　　英検 ® GTEC®

Make the correct choice to complete each sentence. (各2点)

1. You should (　　　) studying to pass the examination.

① be　　　　　　② do　　　　　　③ keep　　　　　　④ stop

2. Are you (　　　) of ghosts?

① afraid　　　　② angry　　　　③ awake　　　　④ good

3. Ayato (　　　) Yamanote Junior High School.

① graduated　　　　　　　　② graduated from

③ was graduating　　　　　　④ was graduating from

4. Our school is famous (　　　) its large schoolyard.

① by　　　　　　② for　　　　　　③ from　　　　　　④ of

5. The boy was good at (　　　) pictures.

① paint　　　　② painting　　　　③ paintings　　　　④ to paint

🎧 Listening　　英文を聞いて理解しよう【知識・技能】【思考力・判断力・表現力】　　共通テスト CD 1

Listen to the English and make the best choice to match the content. (4点)

① The speaker hates making mistakes.

② The speaker is a junior high school student.

③ The speaker isn't afraid of failure anymore.

💬 Interaction　　英文を聞いて会話を続けよう【知識・技能】【思考力・判断力・表現力】　スピーキング・トレーナー CD 2

Listen to the English and respond to the last remark. (7点)

［メ モ　　]

アドバイス　あなたがやりたいこと，予定について話してみよう。

💬 Production (Speak)　　自分の考えを話して伝えよう【思考力・判断力・表現力】　　スピーキング・トレーナー

Speak out your answer to the following question. (7点)

What kind of sports do you like to watch on TV?

アドバイス　単純に質問に答えるだけでなく，その理由などの補足的な発言を加えよう。

Shohei Otani always makes every effort / to **achieve** his dreams. // He gives us some useful hints / for achieving our own dreams. //

① I am the youngest / of three children / in my family. // I was active / in my **childhood**, / and I liked sports / very much. // I enjoyed badminton / and swimming / before I started / to play baseball. //

② My father was a member / of a **nonprofessional** baseball team, / and my older brother / also played baseball. // I joined a local baseball team / when I was seven years old. // This was the beginning / of my love / for baseball. //

③ My father was a coach / of my team, / so he taught me / how to practice. // He always told me / to learn the **basics** / of playing baseball. // Thanks to his advice, / I was able to become a better player. // (130 words)

🔊 音読しよう

スピーキング・トレーナー

Practice 1　スラッシュ位置で文を区切って読んでみよう ☐
Practice 2　英語の強弱のリズムに注意して読んでみよう ☐
TRY!　　　 1分20秒以内に本文全体を音読しよう ☐

📖 **Reading**　本文の内容を読んで理解しよう【知識・技能】【思考力・判断力・表現力】　共通テスト

Make the correct choice to complete each sentence or answer each question. (各4点)

1. Which of the following is true about Shohei Otani and his family? ☐
   ① He doesn't have any younger brothers or sisters.
   ② He has a younger brother.
   ③ His brother played badminton, not baseball.
   ④ His father knew the coach of his baseball team.

2. Shohei Otani began baseball probably because ☐ .
   ① he wanted to achieve his dream
   ② he was tired of badminton and swimming
   ③ his family members played baseball
   ④ his father played baseball as a professional player

3. Shohei Otani thinks that ☐ .
   ① he needed more advice to play baseball better
   ② his coach played baseball like his father did
   ③ his father should tell him how to practice
   ④ his father's advice was useful to become a good player

英語の強弱のリズムを理解して音読することができる。　　大谷選手の幼少期に関する英文を読んで概要や要点を捉えることができる。
文脈を理解して適切な語句を用いて英文を完成することができる。　　平易な英語で話される短い英文を聞いて必要な情報を聞き取ることができる。
家族について簡単な語句を用いて説明することができる。　　好きな勉強場所について簡単な語句を用いて考えを表現することができる。

oals

🔍 Vocabulary & Grammar　重要表現や文法事項について理解しよう【知識】　英検® GTEC®

Make the correct choice to complete each sentence.（各2点）

1. I prepared a practice plan to (　　　　) my goals.
   ① achieve　　　　② agree　　　　③ bring　　　　④ discover

2. Finally, I could solve the difficult problem (　　　　) to her help.
   ① enough　　　　② in order　　　　③ thanks　　　　④ used

3. It is necessary for him to study the (　　　　) of mathematics.
   ① back　　　　② base　　　　③ basics　　　　④ beginner

4. I have a lot of happy memories from my (　　　　).
   ① childhood　　　　② dreams　　　　③ future　　　　④ young

5. The teacher showed the international students (　　　　) the kanji characters.
   ① how reading　　　　② how to read　　　　③ to reading　　　　④ to read how

🎧 Listening　英文を聞いて理解しよう【知識・技能】【思考力・判断力・表現力】　共通テスト　CD 3

Listen to the English and make the best choice to match the content.（4点）

① Both the speaker and her friend were very active.

② The speaker and her friend played soccer with boys.

③ The speaker's friend joined a soccer team, but the speaker didn't.

💬 Interaction　英文を聞いて会話を続けよう【知識・技能】【思考力・判断力・表現力】　スピーキング・トレーナー　CD 4

Listen to the English and respond to the last remark.（7点）

［メモ　　　　　　　　　　　　　　　　　　　　　　　　　　　　　　　　　　　　　］

アドバイス 英語の brother, sister はそれぞれ「兄」と「弟」,「姉」と「妹」の区別がないので, 必要に応じて younger, older などを加えよう。

✏️ Production（Write）　自分の考えを書いて伝えよう【思考力・判断力・表現力】

Write your answer to the following question.（7点）

Where is your favorite place to study?

アドバイス 場所を答えるだけでなく, その理由などを加えるようにしよう。

④　In my high school days, / my coach, / Hiroshi Sasaki, / taught me a **method** / for achieving my goals and dreams. // The method was the use / of a "**Target Achievement Sheet**." // I believe / that it is very important / to decide on a goal / and make it clear. //

⑤　I will teach you / how to make a Target Achievement Sheet. // First, / **divide** a square / into nine equal parts. // Then, / write your final goal / in the **central** square. // In each square / around the central square, / set small targets / to achieve your final goal. // My final goal was / to become a professional baseball player / after high school. //

⑥　I learned the importance / of writing down goals / on paper. // Writing down your goals / can help you / as you try / to achieve them. // (124 words)

◀》 音読しよう　　　　　　　　　　　　　　　　　　　　スピーキング・トレーナー
Practice 1　スラッシュ位置で文を区切って読んでみよう □
Practice 2　英語の強弱のリズムに注意して読んでみよう □
TRY!　　　　1分20秒以内に本文全体を音読しよう □

📖 Reading　本文の内容を読んで理解しよう【知識・技能】【思考力・判断力・表現力】　　　共通テスト

Make the correct choice to complete each sentence or answer each question. (各4点)

1.　Hiroshi Sasaki taught Shohei ☐ .

　　① a method for deciding on his dreams

　　② a subject at high school

　　③ how to achieve his goals and dreams

　　④ how to receive a Target Achievement Sheet

2.　One **opinion** about the Target Achievement Sheet is that ☐ .

　　① it is divided into nine parts

　　② it is important to decide on a goal

　　③ Shohei learned its importance

　　④ the final goal is written in the central square

3.　Which of the following is true about the Target Achievement Sheet? ☐

　　① It has one final goal and nine small targets.

　　② Several final goals are written down in squares.

　　③ Several small targets are around the final goal.

　　④ There is one small target in the central part.

🔍 Vocabulary & Grammar　重要表現や文法事項について理解しよう【知識】　英検® GTEC®

Make the correct choice to complete each sentence. (各2点)

1. Our coach (　　　) the team members into three groups.

① changed　　　② decided　　　③ divided　　　④ reviewed

2. We should decide (　　　) the captain of our soccer team.

① in　　　② into　　　③ on　　　④ to

3. Our (　　　) customers for the new product are high school students.

① focus　　　② goal　　　③ image　　　④ target

4. Our school is proud of the original (　　　) of teaching.

① adventure　　　② control　　　③ method　　　④ pleasure

5. She studies music at university (　　　) a professional violinist.

① becomes　　　② becoming　　　③ to become　　　④ will become

🎧 Listening　英文を聞いて理解しよう【知識・技能】【思考力・判断力・表現力】　共通テスト　CD 5

Listen to the English and make the best choice to match the content. (4点)

① It is necessary for the speaker to change his goal.

② The goal was easy for him to achieve.

③ The speaker is making efforts to achieve his dream.

💬 Interaction　英文を聞いて会話を続けよう【知識・技能】【思考力・判断力・表現力】　スピーキング・トレーナー　CD 6

Listen to the English and respond to the last remark. (7点)

［メモ　　　　　　　　　　　　　　　　　　　　　　　　　　　　　　　　　　　　　　　］

アドバイス　どうしてそう思うのかなどの情報を加えよう。

✏️ Production (Write)　自分の考えを書いて伝えよう【思考力・判断力・表現力】

Write your answer to the following question. (7点)

What is your final goal? And what do you do to achieve it?

アドバイス　ここまでで学んだ to-不定詞や動名詞を積極的に用いて表現しよう。

----

7 What can you do / to achieve your dreams? // I have three important things / to tell you. //

8 First, / you should ask yourself, / "What can I focus on / now?" // When I hurt my leg / and couldn't pitch, / I focused / on batting. // As a result, / I made **remarkable progress** / with my batting skills / during that period. //

9 Second, / you should understand / that failure can lead / to success. // Losing isn't the end. // You should change your **frustration** / into **motivation**. // I believe / that failure can become the **basis** / for success. //

10 Finally, / you should remember / that it is hard / to achieve big dreams. // You will need / to make every effort / and try hard / to achieve them. // Good luck! //

(111 words)

🔊 **音読しよう**　　　　　　　　　　　　　　　　　　　　スピーキング・トレーナー

Practice 1　スラッシュ位置で文を区切って読んでみよう☐
Practice 2　英語の強弱のリズムに注意して読んでみよう☐
TRY!　　　　1分10秒以内に本文全体を音読しよう☐

📖 **Reading**　本文の内容を読んで理解しよう【知識・技能】【思考力・判断力・表現力】　　共通テスト

Make the correct choice to complete each sentence. (各4点)

1. The important things to achieve your dreams are ☐ and ☐. (The order does not matter.)

① to believe that you can succeed without failure

② to know losing can lead to failure

③ to try to change the frustration into motivation

④ to understand that failure can lead to success

2. To achieve your own big dream, you ☐.

① should give up trying hard

② shouldn't focus on pitching

③ may sometimes have a hard time

④ must have the motivation to ask yourself a question

3. One **opinion** from Shohei Otani's message is that ☐.

① achieving big dreams is hard

② he focused on batting when he couldn't pitch

③ he made remarkable progress with his batting skills

④ three important things were said by him

🔊 英語の強弱のリズムを理解して音読することができる。　📖 夢の実現に関する英文を読んで概要や要点を捉えることができる。
🔍 文脈を理解して適切な語句を用いて英文を完成することができる。　🎧 平易な英語で話される短い英文を聞いて必要な情報を聞き取ることができる。
💬 ✎ 失敗やいらだちについて簡単な語句を用いて考えを表現することができる。

als

🔍 Vocabulary & Grammar　重要表現や文法事項について理解しよう【知識】　英検® GTEC®

Make the correct choice to complete each sentence. (各2点)

1. It was very windy. (　　　) a result, the airplane couldn't take off.
   ① As　　　　　② At　　　　　③ By　　　　　④ For

2. The workers quickly changed the space (　　　) a closet.
   ① enough　　　② into　　　　③ thanks　　　④ used

3. Bob is making good (　　　) with his skills in snowboarding.
   ① achievement　② improve　　③ progress　　④ success

4. Now, let me (　　　) on the study of grammar.
   ① face　　　　② figure　　　③ focus　　　④ force

5. Would you like to have (　　　)?
   ① drinking something　　　　　② something drinking
   ③ something to drink　　　　　④ to drink something

🎧 Listening　英文を聞いて理解しよう【知識・技能】【思考力・判断力・表現力】　共通テスト　CD 7

Listen to the English and make the best choice to match the content. (4点)

① The speaker didn't go outside of the gym.

② The speaker is doing training in the gym because it's raining.

③ The speaker went outside of the gym after it stopped raining.

💬 Interaction　英文を聞いて会話を続けよう【知識・技能】【思考力・判断力・表現力】　スピーキング・トレーナー　CD 8

Listen to the English and respond to the last remark. (7点)

［メモ　　　　　　　　　　　　　　　　　　　　　　　　　　　　　　　　　　］

アドバイス　相手の意見も参考にしながら，自分の考えをまとめよう。

✎ Production (Write)　自分の考えを書いて伝えよう【思考力・判断力・表現力】

Write your answer to the following question. (7点)

Do you feel frustration at home or school, and when?

アドバイス　「～するとき」とだけ答えると，ぶっきらぼうな印象を与えるかもしれない。「～するとき，いらだち を感じる」のように答えよう。

You found some information / about young Japanese athletes / and a professional / on the Internet. // You are reading / about them / and listening / to them. //

Young Japanese Athletes / and a Professional /

Akane Yamaguchi / is a badminton player. // She was born / on June 6, 1997. // When she was in her third year / of junior high school, / she was **selected** / as the youngest member / of Japan's national badminton team. // In 2018, / she was **ranked** / first / in the world. // Her motto is / "Enjoy playing every game." //

It is important / for you / to do better / than last year. // Great efforts are **essential**. //

Mima Ito / is a table tennis player. // She was born / on October 21, 2000. // In 2018, / she won three gold **medals** / in Japan's national **competition**. // Her **former** partner / for doubles, / Miu Hirano, / is both her good friend / and good **rival**. //

Thanks to my rivals, / I'm able to focus / on playing / now. // I want to thank my coaches, / rivals, / friends / and family / for supporting me / during my **hardships**. //

Sota Fujii / is a professional *shogi* player. // He was born / on July 19, 2002. // On October 1, 2016, / he became a professional / when he was only 14 years old. // In 2018, / he got the seventh-dan / in *shogi*. //

It is very important / for me / to keep finding the best way / to win. // The only way / to experience being a champion / is to become one, / so I always make every effort / to reach the top. // (236 words)

🔊 音読しよう
Practice 1　スラッシュ位置で文を区切って読んでみよう ☐
Practice 2　英語の強弱のリズムに注意して読んでみよう ☐
TRY!　　　2分20秒以内に本文全体を音読しよう ☐

スピーキング・トレーナー

📖 Reading　本文の内容を読んで理解しよう【知識・技能】【思考力・判断力・表現力】　　共通テスト

Make the correct choice to complete each sentence. (各6点)

1. Akane Yamaguchi ☐ .
   ① and her rival, Miu Hirano played badminton games together before
   ② became a number one player in Japan in 2018
   ③ was an elementary school student when chosen as a member of the national team
   ④ was the youngest player on Japan's national team

2. Sota Fujii ☐ .
   ① always enjoys playing *shogi* games　　② and Mima Ito were born in the 2000s
   ③ played as a professional in July 2016　　④ ranked seventh in *shogi* in 2016

🔍 Vocabulary & Grammar　重要表現や文法事項について理解しよう【知識】　英検® GTEC®

Make the correct choice to complete each sentence. (各2点)

1. After a long training period, Emily made her professional (　　　).
① debut　　　　② entrance　　　　③ goal　　　　④ starting

2. I (　　　) from high school and went to university in the U.S.
① graded　　　② graduated　　　③ greeted　　　④ grew

3. He made every (　　　) to support his aged parents.
① decision　　② effort　　　③ mind　　　④ sure

4. This river (　　　) the two countries.
① divides　　② invites　　③ provides　　④ surveys

5. All these roads (　　　) to the center of the city.
① arrive　　② bring　　③ drive　　④ lead

6. My daily workout is (　　　) for half an hour in the morning.
① jog　　② jogs　　③ to jog　　④ to jogging

7. It was easy for them (　　　) a presentation in English.
① made　　② making　　③ to made　　④ to make

8. I hope (　　　) New Zealand very soon.
① be visiting　　② to be visit　　③ to visit　　④ visiting

🎧 Listening　英文を聞いて理解しよう【知識・技能】【思考力・判断力・表現力】　共通テスト CD 9

Listen to the English and make the best choice to match the content. (各4点)

1. What happened to Takefusa in 2017?
① He became eighteen years old.
② He began to play soccer.
③ He moved to Barcelona.
④ His career as a professional soccer player began.

2. How long was Takefusa a professional player in Japan?
① For about a year.
② For about half a year.
③ For about one-and-a-half years.
④ For nearly two-and-a-half years.

3. Which statement is true?
① Takefusa has good English speaking ability.
② Takefusa moved to Barcelona because of his father's work.
③ Takefusa came back to Japan when he was ten.
④ Takefusa lived in Barcelona for more than two years.

/40

You found a Q&A site / about the Japanese bento. //

I'm planning to travel / to Japan / next week / and want to try some bentos. // Any suggestions? // Lilly //

1 day ago // 3 answers //

You should visit / a Japanese convenience store. // Each store has a large section / for bentos, / and you can choose one / from a wide **variety**. // You can see / some **typical** Japanese foods, / such as sushi, / noodles / and curry. // Victor //

3 hours ago //

You should try *ekiben*, / or "station bentos." // You can buy them / at stations / for **long-distance** trains. // Buy your bento before boarding / and enjoy it / on the train. // At some stations, / you can buy popular local bentos, / such as a *gyutan* bento / at Sendai Station. // Emily //

6 hours ago //

If you stay in a big city / like Tokyo or Osaka, / you should go to a business area / on your lunch break. // A lot of restaurants sell bentos / to business people. // They are made / by a restaurant chef, / but they are not so expensive. // David //

1 day ago // (154 words)

🔊 音読しよう

Practice 1   スラッシュ位置で文を区切って読んでみよう ☐
Practice 2   英語の強弱のリズムに注意して読んでみよう ☐
TRY!   1分40秒以内に本文全体を音読しよう ☐

スピーキング・トレーナー

📖 **Reading**   本文の内容を読んで理解しよう【知識・技能】【思考力・判断力・表現力】   共通テスト

Make the correct choice to complete each sentence or answer each question. (各6点)

1. The person named Lilly [   ].

   ① answers a question

   ② asks a question

   ③ gives suggestions

   ④ tried some bentos in Japan

2. Which is true about Victor, Emily, and David? [   ]

   ① David suggests buying expensive bentos made by a restaurant.

   ② Emily suggests bentos sold on long-distance trains.

   ③ Victor says that we can get sushi at convenience stores in Japan.

   ④ Victor is the first to answer the question among the three.

🔍 Vocabulary & Grammar　重要表現や文法事項について理解しよう【知識】　　英検® GTEC®

Make the correct choice to complete each sentence. (各2点)

1. Bacon, sausage, baked tomato, and sunny-side-up egg are foods for (　　　) English breakfast.
   ① basics　　　② popularly　　　③ tradition　　　④ typical

2. Some plays written by Shakespeare (　　　) as *Romeo and Juliet* or *Hamlet* are famous all over the world.
   ① example　　　② including　　　③ like　　　④ such

3. A lot of long-(　　　) buses arrive at and depart from Tokyo Station.
   ① distance　　　② line　　　③ term　　　④ time

4. Help yourself to some food and drink. You can choose from a wide (　　　).
   ① ability　　　② activity　　　③ society　　　④ variety

5. I'm looking forward to (　　　) from you soon.
   ① be heard　　　② heard　　　③ hear　　　④ hearing

🎧 Listening　英文を聞いて理解しよう【知識・技能】【思考力・判断力・表現力】　共通テスト CD 10

Listen to the English and make the best choice to match the content. (4点)

① Three people didn't want to eat sushi at Kyoto Station.

② Two people answered on the Q&A site.

③ Two among all the answers tell us to eat sushi at Kyoto Station.

💬 Interaction　英文を聞いて会話を続けよう【知識・技能】【思考力・判断力・表現力】　スピーキング・トレーナー CD 11

Listen to the English and respond to the last remark. (7点)

［メモ　　　］

アドバイス　最初の問いかけは，あなたが言ったと想定する発言です。

💬 Production (Speak)　自分の考えを話して伝えよう【思考力・判断力・表現力】　スピーキング・トレーナー

Speak out your answer to the following question. (7点)

Imagine you don't have anything to eat at home and want to eat a bento. Where do you go to buy a bento?

アドバイス　場所を答えるだけでなく，理由なども加えよう。

The Japanese bento is growing popular overseas. // Many **non-Japanese** are enjoying making and eating bentos. // Why are they interested in this Japanese-style box lunch? //

1 "Do you want to take miso soup / with you for lunch? // Do you use a **microwave**?" // A French man is talking / to a young **couple** / in his Japanese **lunchbox** shop / in Kyoto. // He is one of the many foreign people / **fascinated** by Japanese bento culture. // He is selling Japanese lunchboxes / to travelers / in the shop. // He is also selling them / to people abroad / through the Internet. //

2 Many people in other countries / are surprised to know / that the Japanese bento is beautiful. // In a typical bento, / a variety of **bite-sized** foods / are **neatly arranged** / into a lunchbox. // It is very colorful / and looks like a work of art. // More and more people / want to try making this art. //

3 In addition, / the bento is healthy. // It usually **contains** many foods, / like rice, / meat, / fish, / vegetables / and fruit. // It is a **full-course** meal / in a small box. // (168 words)

◀)) **音読しよう**　　　　　　　　　　　　　　　　　　　スピーキング・トレーナー

Practice 1　スラッシュ位置で文を区切って読んでみよう □
Practice 2　英語の強弱のリズムに注意して読んでみよう □
TRY!　　　　1分40秒以内に本文全体を音読しよう □

📖 **Reading**　本文の内容を読んで理解しよう【知識・技能】【思考力・判断力・表現力】　　共通テスト

Make the correct choice to complete each sentence or answer each question. (各4点)

1. A French man in the first paragraph is 　　　.
   ① doing business in France　　　② running a shop selling lunchboxes
   ③ traveling around Japan　　　　④ working in a box lunch shop in Kyoto

2. A typical Japanese bento is beautiful because 　　　.
   ① bite-sized foods are in a colorful lunchbox
   ② foods used for it are healthy
   ③ it is similar to a full-course meal in a restaurant
   ④ some kinds of foods are arranged like a work of art

3. Which question is **not** answered in the paragraphs? 　　　
   ① For what purpose is the Internet used by the lunchbox shop?
   ② What does a typical Japanese bento look like?
   ③ When did the French man start to work?
   ④ Who is the French man talking to?

🔍 Vocabulary & Grammar 　重要表現や文法事項について理解しよう【知識】　　　英検® GTEC®

Make the correct choice to complete each sentence. (各2点)

1. From a great (　　　) of shoes here, you will be able to find your favorite ones.
   ① variation　　　② varieties　　　③ variety　　　④ various

2. Companies are developing (　　　) smartphones to meet the new mobile communication system.
   ① many and many　② more and more　③ more many　④ much and much

3. Hundreds of (　　　) go on a date to the amusement park every year.
   ① couples　　　② pairs　　　③ pets　　　④ twins

4. Her grandfather was a great baseball player, and (　　　) addition, a famous musician.
   ① by　　　② in　　　③ on　　　④ to

5. He bought a (　　　) because he couldn't buy a new one.
   ① piano used　　② piano using　　③ used piano　　④ using piano

🎧 Listening 　英文を聞いて理解しよう【知識・技能】【思考力・判断力・表現力】　共通テスト　CD 12

Listen to the English and make the best choice to match the content. (4点)

① The lunchbox was bought by the speaker living in Tokyo.

② The lunchbox was bought for the speaker's friend in Paris.

③ The lunchbox was bought for the speaker's friend living in Tokyo.

💬 Interaction 　英文を聞いて会話を続けよう【知識・技能】【思考力・判断力・表現力】 スピーキング・トレーナー CD 13

Listen to the English and respond to the last remark. (7点)

［メモ　　　］

アドバイス　だれがあなたに話しかけているのかを想像して答えよう。

✐ Production（Write）　自分の考えを書いて伝えよう【思考力・判断力・表現力】

Write your answer to the following question. (7点)

What is your lunchbox like? If you don't have one, what kind of lunchbox do you want?

アドバイス　あなたの弁当箱の特徴をよく思い出して，説明してみよう。

----

④　The idea of bringing bentos / to school or work / is not **unique** / to Japan. //

⑤　**Dutch** people prepare lunches / of simple ham or cheese sandwiches, / along with some fruit, / like an apple or a banana. // They make sandwiches / for themselves, / and it is not common / to prepare them / for someone else. //

⑥　American people put sandwiches, / fruit, / a small **carton** of juice, / and sometimes snacks / into a lunchbox. // There are a variety of sandwiches, / but **peanut** butter and **jelly** sandwiches / have been popular / among children / for a long time. //

⑦　The Chinese-style box lunch / contains rice / covered with one or two main dishes, / such as **stir-fried** vegetables. // Chinese people use **containers** / to carry bentos, / and they always warm the box lunch up / before they eat it. // This is because they don't like to eat cold food. //　(133 words)

🔊 **音読しよう**

スピーキング・トレーナー

Practice 1　スラッシュ位置で文を区切って読んでみよう ☐
Practice 2　英語の強弱のリズムに注意して読んでみよう ☐
TRY!　　　　1分20秒以内に本文全体を音読しよう ☐

📖 **Reading**　本文の内容を読んで理解しよう【知識・技能】【思考力・判断力・表現力】　　共通テスト

Make the correct choice to complete each sentence or answer each question. (各4点)

1.　Which of the following are true about Dutch people? (Choose two options. The order does not matter.) ☐ ・ ☐

　① They usually don't prepare a bento for their son or daughter.

　② They like sandwiches with peanut butter and jelly.

　③ They put some fruit into their sandwiches.

　④ They take out simple sandwiches for their lunch.

2.　Many American children like ☐ in their sandwiches.

　① to put some fruit

　② to put ham or cheese

　③ to put peanut butter

　④ to put stir-fried vegetables

3.　☐ are least likely to put a fresh salad in their lunch box.

　① American people

　② Chinese people

　③ Dutch people

　④ Japanese people

🔍 Vocabulary & Grammar　重要表現や文法事項について理解しよう【知識】　英検® GTEC®

Make the correct choice to complete each sentence. （各2点）

1. This laptop computer sells well. This is (　　　) it provides excellent cost performance.
   ① because　② how　③ when　④ why

2. The garden was (　　　) fallen leaves.
   ① covered with　② covered in　③ covering　④ covering of

3. The artist created some watercolor paintings, (　　　) a lot of oil paintings.
   ① addition to　② along with　③ including　④ such as

4. I like to put (　　　) on toast better than butter.
   ① gel　② glue　③ jelly　④ jewel

5. Anne is absent today. She (　　　) sick since last week.
   ① has been　② is　③ is being　④ was

🎧 Listening　英文を聞いて理解しよう【知識・技能】【思考力・判断力・表現力】　共通テスト CD 14

Listen to the English and make the best choice to match the content. （4点）

① The speaker has eaten French-style bentos many times.
② The speaker has read magazines having pictures of French-style bentos.
③ The speaker hasn't read a book about French box lunches.

💬 Interaction　英文を聞いて会話を続けよう【知識・技能】【思考力・判断力・表現力】　スピーキング・トレーナー CD 15

Listen to the English and respond to the last remark. （7点）

［メモ　　　　　　　　　　　　　　　　　　　　　　　　　　　　　　　　　］

アドバイス　相手が期待している返答をしてあげよう。

✏️ Production（Write）　自分の考えを書いて伝えよう【思考力・判断力・表現力】

Write your answer to the following question. （7点）

Which do you want to eat, a Dutch, American, or Chinese box lunch? And why?

アドバイス　自分がなぜその国の弁当を選んだのかわかりやすく伝えよう。

⑧　Japanese **homemade** bentos are full of love. // In Japan, / many high school students eat a bento / made by their parents / for lunch. // The parents get up early / in the morning / and make their bentos. // "Will my son like these side dishes?" // "Is this bento **well-balanced** for my daughter?" // They always think about such things / while they are making bentos. //

⑨　*Kyaraben*, / or "character bentos," / are created from parents' love. // They want to make the food **attractive** / and encourage their kids / to eat **properly**. // Their kids are able to eat / even their least favorite foods. //

⑩　Japanese parents put messages / into the bentos, / and the children receive them. // Some people in other countries / have noticed this **function** of bentos, / and they also enjoy making them. // Japanese-style bentos / can be a remarkable communication tool / around the world. //　(133 words)

◀)) 音読しよう

スピーキング・トレーナー

Practice 1　スラッシュ位置で文を区切って読んでみよう ☐
Practice 2　英語の強弱のリズムに注意して読んでみよう ☐
TRY!　　　 1分20秒以内に本文全体を音読しよう ☐

📖 **Reading**　本文の内容を読んで理解しよう【知識・技能】【思考力・判断力・表現力】　共通テスト

Make the correct choice to complete each sentence or answer each question. (各4点)

1. Japanese parents are thinking the following when they make bentos: ☐ .
   ① the bentos should be well-balanced
   ② their children shouldn't eat them up
   ③ their children will love themselves
   ④ their children won't have to wash dishes

2. Thanks to *Kyaraben*, children ☐ .
   ① are able to be attractive after eating them
   ② are encouraged to feel their parents' love
   ③ can't eat their most favorite food
   ④ don't mind eating their least favorite foods in a bento

3. Which of the following is true about Japanese-style bentos? ☐
   ① Messages for parents are sometimes put into them.
   ② People in other countries can't understand their unique functions.
   ③ Some foreign people know that they sometimes carry messages.
   ④ They are widely used for communication around the world.

- 英語の強弱のリズムを理解して音読することができる。
- 文脈を理解して適切な語句を用いて英文を完成することができる。
- 自分の弁当について簡単な語句を用いて説明することができる。
- 日本の手作り弁当に関する英文を読んで概要や要点を捉えることができる。
- 平易な英語で話される短い英文を聞いて必要な情報を聞き取ることができる。
- キャラ弁について簡単な語句を用いて説明することができる。

Vocabulary & Grammar　重要表現や文法事項について理解しよう【知識】　英検® GTEC®

Make the correct choice to complete each sentence. (各2点)

1. One of the (　　　) of zoos is to protect endangered animals.
   ① facilities　　② functions　　③ homes　　④ places

2. These new sports wears will become (　　　) to young athletes.
   ① attract　　② attraction　　③ attractive　　④ attractively

3. If you don't use the machine (　　　), it will break.
   ① politely　　② probably　　③ promptly　　④ properly

4. My friend (　　　) me to talk to international students in English.
   ① encouraged　　② expressed　　③ influenced　　④ introduced

5. The man (　　　) his report, so he's free now.
   ① has finishing　　② hasn't finished　　③ has written　　④ has wrote

Listening　英文を聞いて理解しよう【知識・技能】【思考力・判断力・表現力】　共通テスト　CD 16

Listen to the English and make the best choice to match the content. (4点)

① The speaker took a bento to school when he was a junior high school student.

② The speaker wanted to take a bento when he was a junior high school student.

③ The speaker's junior high school had a school lunch service.

Interaction　英文を聞いて会話を続けよう【知識・技能】【思考力・判断力・表現力】　スピーキング・トレーナー　CD 17

Listen to the English and respond to the last remark. (7点)

[メモ　　　　　　　　　　　　　　　　　　　　　　　　　　]

アドバイス　質問に対する「はい」か「いいえ」の返答を忘れないようにしよう。

Production (Write)　自分の考えを書いて伝えよう【思考力・判断力・表現力】

Write your answer to the following question. (7点)

Does your mother or father sometimes make a *kyaraben* for you?

アドバイス　Yes か No だけでは終わらず，補足情報を加えるようにしよう。

21

You are interested / in joining a bento contest. // You are looking at a **leaflet** / about it. //
International Bento Contest 2025 //

The White Snow Bento Company / has held an International Bento Contest / since 2016. // The 10th contest will start / on April 25, / 2025. // The **theme** this year is / "a bento using **locally**-produced foods." // The first-prize winner / will get a pair of **round-trip** tickets / to Hokkaido / from his/her country. // We hope / that you will take part in this contest! //

Contest Rules //

Entry Period: / From April 25 / to May 6, / 2025 //

Theme //　　　　　A bento / using locally-produced foods //

How to Enter //　　Fill out the entry form, / and **submit** your recipe and pictures / through the contest website. //

· Take two pictures. // One should be a picture / of all foods before cooking, / and the other should be a picture / of the **completed** bento. //

Entry Conditions //　　You must be 15 or older / to join the contest. //

For more information, / visit our website / at https://www.wsbc.com/2025/contest/ //

(163 words)

🔊 **音読しよう**　　　　　　　　　　　　　　　　　　スピーキング・トレーナー
　Practice 1　スラッシュ位置で文を区切って読んでみよう ☐
　Practice 2　英語の強弱のリズムに注意して読んでみよう ☐
　TRY!　　　　1分40秒以内に本文全体を音読しよう ☐

📖 **Reading**　本文の内容を読んで理解しよう【知識・技能】【思考力・判断力・表現力】　　共通テスト

Make the correct choice to complete each sentence. (各6点)

1.　The International Bento Contest ☐ .
　① has been held once a year since 2016
　② has had the same theme since its beginning
　③ will present the winner a package tour to Hokkaido
　④ will receive entries only from Japan

2.　The White Snow Bento Company will accept an entry ☐ .
　① form mailed to the company on May 1
　② made by a fifteen-year-old girl
　③ of party food using locally-produced foods
　④ with a recipe and two different pictures of the finished bento

🔎 Vocabulary & Grammar　重要表現や文法事項について理解しよう【知識】　英検® GTEC®

Make the correct choice to complete each sentence. (各2点)

1. My mother gave me (　　　) for my last birthday.
   ① a pair of earring　　　　　　　② a pair of earrings
   ③ an earring pair　　　　　　　　④ pairs of earring

2. I (　　　) Beth's birthday party yesterday. She looked very happy.
   ① took care of　② took part in　③ took place　④ took out

3. Could you (　　　) out the card? You need your name, home address, and cellphone number.
   ① fell　　　　　② file　　　　　③ fill　　　　　④ full

4. I use two different lunchboxes. One is for rice and side dishes, (　　　) is for sandwiches.
   ① another　　　② others　　　③ the other　　　④ the others

5. My favorite movie is *Mission Impossible*. That was (　　　)!
   ① a movie exciting　② an exciting movie　③ excited a movie　④ exciting a movie

6. The (　　　) next to Mary is my cousin.
   ① girl standing　② girl is standing　③ standing girl　④ stood girl

7. My brother (　　　) the train this morning. So he was late for the first class.
   ① missed　　② has missed　　③ have missed　　④ will miss

8. Have you ever (　　　) a foreign country?
   ① been　　② been to　　③ been with　　④ go to

🎧 Listening　英文を聞いて理解しよう【知識・技能】【思考力・判断力・表現力】　共通テスト CD 18

Listen to the English and make the best choice to match the content. (各4点)

1. What did the speaker want to know on the Internet?
   ① Bookstores selling history books.　　② The first *ekiben* in history.
   ③ The first railway service.　　　　　　④ The history of Yokohama.

2. Where was the first railway service opened in Japan?
   ① At Ueno Station.　　　　　　　② At Utsunomiya Station.
   ③ Between Ueno Station and Osaka Station.
   ④ Between Shimbashi Station and Yokohama Station.

3. Which statement is true about the talk?
   ① No station bentos are sold at Osaka and Ueno Stations now.
   ② The first *ekiben*, or station bentos, were sold at Yokohama Station.
   ③ The speaker learned about the *ekiben* of Utsunomiya Station from a history book.
   ④ We don't know which station sold the first *ekiben* in history.

You want to learn some information / about cellphones and public phones. // You are listening to a presentation / about them. //

The total numbers of cellphones and public phones / in Japan / from 1990 to 2017 //

　　The graph shows the changes / in the total numbers / of cellphones and public phones / in Japan / from 1990 to 2017. //

　　As you can see, / before 1993, / cellphones were not very common. // From 1999 to 2008, / the total number of cellphones increased / by more than 100%. // In 2011, / there were more than 120 million cellphones. // This means / that the number of cellphones / was greater / than the **population** / of Japan. // Even today, / the number is increasing / year by year. //

　　On the other hand, / from 1990 to 2017, / the number of public phones **decreased** / by more than 80%. // Will the number of public phones / continue to decrease / year by year? // (140 words)

🔊 **音読しよう**　　　　　　　　　　　　　　　　　　　　スピーキング・トレーナー

Practice 1　スラッシュ位置で文を区切って読んでみよう☐
Practice 2　英語の強弱のリズムに注意して読んでみよう☐
TRY!　　　　1分20秒以内に本文全体を音読しよう☐

📖 **Reading**　本文の内容を読んで理解しよう【知識・技能】【思考力・判断力・表現力】　　共通テスト

Make the correct choice to complete each sentence or answer each question. (各4点)

1. Before 1993, cellphones were ☐ .
   ① more popular than public phones　② not invented
   ③ not so popular　④ too heavy to use

2. Which of the following is true? ☐
   ① Cellphones have always been popular since their debut.
   ② Cellphones have gained popularity since the beginning of the 20th century.
   ③ The number of public phones in 2017 was much smaller than that in 1990.
   ④ The number of cellphones began to decrease greatly in 2011.

3. What is **not** known from the graph mentioned in the passage? ☐
   ① The change in the number of cellphones for more than 15 years.
   ② The number of cellphones in 1990.
   ③ The number of public phones in 1990.
   ④ The population of Japan.

🔍 Vocabulary & Grammar　重要表現や文法事項について理解しよう【知識】　英検® GTEC®

Make the correct choice to complete each sentence. (各2点)

1. The (　　　　) of elderly people in this town is increasing.
   ① age　　　　　② figure　　　　　③ number　　　　　④ sign

2. As you (　　　　), the machine is very heavy.
   ① see　　　　　② glance　　　　　③ look at　　　　　④ watch

3. Year (　　　　) year, my eyesight is getting weak.
   ① and　　　　　② by　　　　　③ or　　　　　④ to

4. The (　　　　) of Japan is more than 120 million.
   ① people　　　　② person　　　　③ popularity　　　④ population

5. The map (　　　　) the evacuation sites around the town.
   ① has shown　　② is showing　　③ show　　　④ shows

🎧 Listening　英文を聞いて理解しよう【知識・技能】【思考力・判断力・表現力】　共通テスト　CD 19

Listen to the English and make the best choice to match the content. (4点)

① The speaker didn't have a cellphone when she entered high school.

② The speaker doesn't want a cellphone.

③ The speaker got her first cellphone when she was a junior high school student.

💬 Interaction　英文を聞いて会話を続けよう【知識・技能】【思考力・判断力・表現力】　スピーキング・トレーナー　CD 20

Listen to the English and respond to the last remark. (7点)

〔メモ　　　　　　　　　　　　　　　　　　　　　　　　　　　　　　　　　　〕

アドバイス　あなたが携帯電話をよく使う場面を考えよう。

💬 Production (Speak)　自分の考えを話して伝えよう【思考力・判断力・表現力】　スピーキング・トレーナー

Speak out your answer to the following question. (7点)

Have you ever used a public phone? Do you want to use one?

アドバイス　No の場合でも必ず理由をそえるようにしよう。

Can you live / without your cellphone? // Most people use their cellphones / for various purposes. // The **evolution** of the cellphone / over the last 50 years / is an amazing story. //

① A lot of things have happened / in the last 50 years. // When it comes to technology, / "50 years ago" / is like ancient times. // What has **evolved** / surprisingly fast / as technology has developed? // Yes, / it's the cellphone. //

② **Nowadays**, / seven billion cellphones are used / around the world. // Who invented the cellphone? // It was Dr. Martin Cooper, / an engineer / at a **telecommunications** company / in the U.S. //

③ Cooper invented the first cellphone / in 1973. // He wanted to make a phone / which people could carry / with them anywhere. // The first model / was 22.5 centimeters long / and **weighed** about one kilogram. // The **battery** lasted / only 20 minutes. //

④ In 1973, / Cooper stood on a street / in New York / and made a phone call. // He said, / "I'm calling / from a cellphone! // A real **handheld**, / **portable** cellphone!" //

(156 words)

🔊 **音読しよう**

Practice 1　スラッシュ位置で文を区切って読んでみよう ☐
Practice 2　英語の強弱のリズムに注意して読んでみよう ☐
TRY!　　　　1分30秒以内に本文全体を音読しよう ☐

スピーキング・トレーナー

📖 **Reading**　本文の内容を読んで理解しよう【知識・技能】【思考力・判断力・表現力】　　共通テスト

Make the correct choice to complete each sentence or answer each question. (各4点)

1. In the field of technology, half a century ago is ☐.
   ① far from the ancient days　　② far from the present day
   ③ like the present day　　　　　④ not very old at all

2. About seven billion cellphones ☐.
   ① are now in use all over the world
   ② go into the market every year
   ③ have been used for 50 years
   ④ were thrown away last year

3. Which of the following is **not** true about the cellphone invented in 1973? ☐
   ① A US company engineer made efforts to develop it.
   ② Its inventor, Dr. Cooper, received a phone call on a street in New York.
   ③ People could use it for about twenty minutes without recharging it.
   ④ The first cellphone invented by Dr. Cooper weighed one kilogram.

26

🔍 Vocabulary & Grammar　重要表現や文法事項について理解しよう【知識】　英検® GTEC®

Make the correct choice to complete each sentence. （各2点）

1. (　　　　　), people can know the daily lives of movie actors easily through their posts on social media.

   ① Always　　　　② Early　　　　③ Nowadays　　　　④ Right now

2. When it (　　　　) to tennis, Judy is the best in her class.

   ① comes　　　　② gets　　　　③ goes　　　　④ turns

3. Laptop computers ten years ago often (　　　　　) more than two kilograms.

   ① had　　　　② waited　　　　③ weighed　　　　④ made

4. When remote controllers don't work correctly, try to change (　　　　) first.

   ① air conditioners　② batteries　　　③ energy　　　④ power cords

5. I have met a woman (　　　　) husband is a doctor.

   ① which　　　　② who　　　　③ whom　　　　④ whose

🎧 Listening　英文を聞いて理解しよう【知識・技能】【思考力・判断力・表現力】　共通テスト　CD 21

Listen to the English and make the best choice to match the content. （4点）

① The speaker has owned three cellphones including the present one.

② The speaker is now using four different cellphones.

③ The speaker used three cellphones before the one he has now.

💬 Interaction　英文を聞いて会話を続けよう【知識・技能】【思考力・判断力・表現力】　スピーキング・トレーナー　CD 22

Listen to the English and respond to the last remark. （7点）

［メモ　　　　　　　　　　　　　　　　　　　　　　　　　　　　　　　　　　　　]

　アドバイス　冒頭の疑問詞をよく聞き，何を答えるべきか考えよう。

🖉 Production（Write）　自分の考えを書いて伝えよう【思考力・判断力・表現力】

Write your answer to the following question. （7点）

Do you pay the cellphone bill by yourself? Do you think it's expensive?

　アドバイス　自分が支払っていない場合でも，料金について何か書くようにしよう。

------

⑤ The first cellphone / for public use / was **released** / on the market / in 1983. // It was only for talking. // Its screen was so small / that it was not easy / to use the cellphone. // Since then, / telecommunications companies / have put their efforts / into adding other functions, / along with the talking function. //

⑥ In 2000, / a camera function was added / to cellphones. // The **quality** of the images was low, / so people at that time / thought of it / as an **extra**. // Then, / "the **wallet** cellphone" was introduced / in 2004. // Thanks to it, / people could buy things / with their cellphones. // As various **features** were added, / screens became bigger / and cellphones became easier to use. // People came to use cellphones / instead of other **devices**, / such as dictionaries and music players. //

⑦ Cellphones are not just for talking anymore. // They are portable devices. // Companies have developed various **applications** / and have changed cellphones / into **toolboxes** / with a **solution** / for almost every need. // (152 words)

◀) 音読しよう

スピーキング・トレーナー

Practice 1　スラッシュ位置で文を区切って読んでみよう☐
Practice 2　英語の強弱のリズムに注意して読んでみよう☐
TRY!　　　1分30秒以内に本文全体を音読しよう☐

📖 **Reading**　本文の内容を読んで理解しよう【知識・技能】【思考力・判断力・表現力】　共通テスト

Make the correct choice to complete each sentence or answer each question. (各4点)

1. Before 1983, the cellphone ☐ for ordinary people.
   ① was already common
   ② was part of life
   ③ wasn't released
   ④ wasn't as expensive as it is now

2. Which of the following is true about the function of the cellphone? ☐
   ① After 2000, an extra screen was added to the camera.
   ② The camera function was not introduced until 2000.
   ③ The talking function doesn't remain now.
   ④ The wallet function was added between 2000 and 2003.

3. One **opinion** about the cellphones now is that ☐.
   ① some people use them to listen to music
   ② they are easy to use
   ③ they can be used for shopping
   ④ they have other functions besides talking

🔍 Vocabulary & Grammar　　重要表現や文法事項について理解しよう【知識】　　　英検® GTEC®

Make the correct choice to complete each sentence. (各2点)

1. She (　　　　) more cheese to her pasta.
   ① added　　　　　② ate　　　　　　③ fell　　　　　　④ had

2. One of the (　　　　) of the pool here is its latest water cleaning system.
   ① creatures　　　② features　　　③ futures　　　④ natures

3. This type of airplane is (　　　　) large that it can carry more than 500 people.
   ① much　　　　　② so　　　　　　③ too　　　　　　④ very

4. Early in the next year, the band is going to (　　　　) its best album.
   ① realize　　　　② release　　　③ rescue　　　④ research

5. A chairperson is a person who (　　　　) a meeting.
   ① lead　　　　　② leading　　　③ leads　　　④ led

🎧 Listening　　英文を聞いて理解しよう【知識・技能】【思考力・判断力・表現力】　　共通テスト　CD 23

Listen to the English and make the best choice to match the content. (4点)

① The quality of the speaker's cellphone camera is good enough.

② The speaker thinks his cellphone camera isn't as good as his other camera.

③ The speaker wants to buy a cellphone with a higher quality camera.

💬 Interaction　　英文を聞いて会話を続けよう【知識・技能】【思考力・判断力・表現力】　スピーキング・トレーナー　CD 24

Listen to the English and respond to the last remark. (7点)

[メモ　　　　　　　　　　　　　　　　　　　　　　　　　　　　　　　　　　]

アドバイス　あなたがそのアプリをどの程度利用するのかについても考えよう。

✍ Production (Write)　　自分の考えを書いて伝えよう【思考力・判断力・表現力】

Write your answer to the following question. (7点)

Are you happy with your cellphone? Do you want a new cellphone?

アドバイス　答えが Yes/No にかかわらず，その理由となるような情報もそえるようにしよう。

----

⑧ Smartphones were introduced / in 2007. // Today, / most people have a smartphone. // Some people **expect** / that smartphones will **eventually** take over the cellphone market. //

⑨ The cellphone has been evolving **rapidly** / in the past **decade**. // Both its **appearance** and purpose / have changed / during that time. // People need more functions / on their cellphones, / and companies are trying / to meet their needs. // The evolution of the cellphone / is an important event / in the history / of telecommunications technology. //

⑩ In the future, / cellphones will go through / another big change. // It is expected / that we will not need / a **physical** screen / at all / in the near future. // It is thought / that we will be able to **link** the devices / to our brain / and control them / with our thoughts. // This will be a **technologically-assisted** form / of **telepathy**. //

⑪ What do you think / the future phone will look like? // You may wonder, / "How will we change the cellphone?" // The real question is, / "How will the cellphone change us?" // (158 words)

🔊 **音読しよう**　　　　　　　　　　　　　　　　　　　　スピーキング・トレーナー
Practice 1　スラッシュ位置で文を区切って読んでみよう □
Practice 2　英語の強弱のリズムに注意して読んでみよう □
TRY!　　　　1分30秒以内に本文全体を音読しよう □

📖 **Reading**　本文の内容を読んで理解しよう【知識・技能】【思考力・判断力・表現力】　　共通テスト

Make the correct choice to complete each sentence or answer each question. (各4点)

1. In 2007, smartphones _____ .

    ① introduced us to the cellphone market

    ② joined the cellphone market

    ③ pushed the old type of cellphones away

    ④ filled the cellphone market

2. According to paragraph 9, we can know _____ .

    ① how the shape of the cellphone has changed

    ② what customers want for the cellphones

    ③ what kind of functions people need for their cellphones

    ④ when designers of the cellphone answered people's needs

3. Which of the following is **not** likely to be the feature of the future cellphone? _____

    ① Its user will not need to touch the screen when he/she uses it.

    ② It will be controlled directly by the thoughts of its user.

    ③ It will be able to catch the signals from its user's brain.

    ④ It will have a small screen to show its user's thoughts.

- 英語の強弱のリズムを理解して音読することができる。
- 文脈を理解して適切な語句を用いて英文を完成することができる。
- よく使うアプリについて簡単な語句を用いて説明することができる。
- 携帯電話のさらなる発展に関する英文を読んで概要や要点を捉えることができる。
- 平易な英語で話される短い英文を聞いて必要な情報を聞き取ることができる。
- 自分の携帯電話について簡単な語句を用いて説明することができる。

oals

Vocabulary & Grammar　　重要表現や文法事項について理解しよう【知識】　　英検® GTEC®

Make the correct choice to complete each sentence. (各2点)

1. He has been paying more attention to his (　　　) recently.　He wears stylish clothes.

    ① activity　　　　② amusement　　　③ appearance　　　④ approach

2. Mr. Sakai took (　　　) Mr. Ito's position as a coach of the baseball club last month.

    ① after　　　　　② over　　　　　　③ part in　　　　　④ place

3. He speaks English so fast that I couldn't understand him (　　　).

    ① at all　　　　　② by all　　　　　③ in all　　　　　④ of all

4. I (　　　) that he would win first prize, but he lost in his first game.

    ① decided　　　　② excited　　　　③ expected　　　　④ managed

5. Meg has (　　　) the piano since 8:00 this morning.

    ① be play　　　　　② been played　　　③ been playing　　　④ playing

Listening　　英文を聞いて理解しよう【知識・技能】【思考力・判断力・表現力】　　共通テスト　CD 25

Listen to the English and make the best choice to match the content. (4点)

    ① The cellphone is kept clean by a soft silicon case.

    ② The orange smartphone case protects the cellphone.

    ③ The smartphone is protected with a clear case.

Interaction　　英文を聞いて会話を続けよう【知識・技能】【思考力・判断力・表現力】　スピーキング・トレーナー　CD 26

Listen to the English and respond to the last remark. (7点)

〔メモ　　　　　　　　　　　　　　　　　　　　　　　　　　　　　　　　　　　　　　〕

アドバイス　用途や理由を付け加えるようにしよう。

Production (Write)　　自分の考えを書いて伝えよう【思考力・判断力・表現力】

Write your answer to the following question. (7点)

How long have you been using your cellphone?　Where did you buy it?

アドバイス　使用期間と購入場所を明確に書こう。

Koji and Airi are making a presentation / about their ideas / for a future phone. //

"A Special **Contact Lens**" //

Hi. // I'm Koji. // My idea for a future phone / is a lens type of phone. // I named it / "A Special Contact Lens." //

You can wear a lens / in your eye / like a **normal** contact lens. // The lens can catch / your brain waves. // When it is necessary, / a screen **automatically** appears / in the air. // Only the user / can see it. // The phone **combines** / several computers / through the Internet. // You can **operate** it / with your thoughts. //

"New Face: Part of My Fashion" //

Hi. // I'm Airi. // Today, / I'm going to tell you / about my idea / for a future phone. // I call it "New Face." // It's part of my fashion. //

The phone is / an **earring** and a **bracelet**. // The earring shows the screen / in front of you. // The bracelet is a Wi-Fi **hub**. // It connects / to the Internet. //

It's a cool future phone! // (157 words)

🔊 **音読しよう**　　　　　　　　　　　　　　　　　　スピーキング・トレーナー

Practice 1　スラッシュ位置で文を区切って読んでみよう ☐
Practice 2　英語の強弱のリズムに注意して読んでみよう ☐
TRY!　　　　１分30秒以内に本文全体を音読しよう ☐

📖 **Reading**　本文の内容を読んで理解しよう【知識・技能】【思考力・判断力・表現力】　　共通テスト

Make the correct choice to complete each sentence. (各6点)

1. A Special Contact Lens ☐ .

    ① can catch the user's brain waves

    ② cannot be used as a phone

    ③ has the same function as the standard contact lens

    ④ is used in both eyes

2. New Face ☐ .

    ① cannot connect to the Internet

    ② consists of two items

    ③ is attached to a human's face

    ④ consists of two earrings and two bracelets

🔍 Vocabulary & Grammar　重要表現や文法事項について理解しよう【知識】　英検® GTEC®

Make the correct choice to complete each sentence. (各2点)

1. You can see a beautiful garden (　　) front of the museum.
   ① at　　　　② in　　　　③ on　　　　④ to

2. Could you show me how to (　　) this printing machine?
   ① combine　　② operate　　③ provide　　④ separate

3. The singer decided to hold a concert (　　) of the canceled one.
   ① afraid　　② full　　③ instead　　④ made up

4. This intelligent bus can run (　　) without a driver.
   ① auto　　② automatic　　③ automatically　　④ automation

5. She is going to (　　) a presentation to her students.
   ① do　　② make　　③ speak　　④ take

6. The problem is very difficult. We can't find any (　　) to it at all.
   ① experience　　② influence　　③ mistake　　④ solution

7. The new action movie (　　) I watched yesterday was not very interesting.
   ① which　　② who　　③ whom　　④ whose

8. The fire (　　) for more than two hours.
   ① has been burn　　② has been burned　　③ has been burning　　④ has burn

🎧 Listening　英文を聞いて理解しよう【知識・技能】【思考力・判断力・表現力】　共通テスト　CD 27

Listen to the English and make the best choice to match the content. (各4点)

1. In 1884, what did the Californian farmer approach?
   ① A cellphone.　　② A computer.
   ③ A smartphone.　　④ A telephone.

2. What did the farmer want to do?
   ① To fix the vibrating plate.
   ② To receive a message.
   ③ To send a piece of paper.
   ④ To talk with a person.

3. Which statement is true?
   ① The farmer got angry because the number he knew was a wrong one.
   ② The farmer seemed to use the phone for the first time.
   ③ The farmer was able to order a hammer and nails.
   ④ The farmer was familiar with how to use the phone.

You are visiting a zoo. // You see giant pandas / and find a notice / in front of their cage. // Also, / you hear an **announcement** / about pandas. //

Giant Pandas //

Height: / Adults can grow / to more than 120 centimeters //

Weight: / 100-150 kilograms /

　　　A baby panda is / about 1/900 the size / of its mother. //

Population: / About 1,800 / in the wild / (about 400 in zoos) //

Habitat: / Bamboo forests / in China //

　　Pandas first came to Ueno Zoo / from China / in 1972 / as a symbol of the friendship / between China and Japan. // A lot of people / went to see them / at the zoo. // In 1994, / a panda came to Wakayama. // There is a research base there / for giant pandas. // More than ten pandas / have been born there. // Pandas are very popular / all over Japan. //

　　This animal / with a black and white coat / is loved / around the world. // Pandas live mainly in bamboo forests / in China. // They must eat / from 10 to 40 kilograms / of bamboo / every day, / and they need 4,000 **kilocalories** / a day / to stay alive. // In order to save energy, / they try not to move much. // They **seem** to move / very slowly, / but pandas are very good at climbing trees. //

　　The panda is special / for World Wide **Fund** for Nature, / or WWF. // It has been WWF's symbol / since its **foundation** / in 1961. // Since then, / the number of pandas / has increased / little by little. // They are symbols / of all **endangered species**. // (235 words)

🔊 **音読しよう**　　　　　　　　　　　　　　　　　スピーキング・トレーナー

Practice 1　スラッシュ位置で文を区切って読んでみよう ☐
Practice 2　イントネーションに注意して読んでみよう ☐
TRY!　　　　2分20秒以内に本文全体を音読しよう ☐

📖 **Reading**　本文の内容を読んで理解しよう【知識・技能】【思考力・判断力・表現力】　　共通テスト

Make the correct choice to answer each question. (各6点)

1. How many pandas are there all around the world? ☐
   ① About 1,400.　　② About 1,800.　　③ Less than 2,000.　　④ More than 2,000.

2. What is **not** known from the announcement? ☐
   ① The amount of food that a panda has to eat a day.
   ② The change in the number of pandas after WWF was founded.
   ③ The location of the research center for giant pandas in Japan.
   ④ The total number of baby pandas which were born in Ueno Zoo.

🔍 Vocabulary & Grammar　重要表現や文法事項について理解しよう【知識】　　英検® GTEC®

Make the correct choice to complete each sentence. (各2点)

1. This kind of monkey is disappearing from the earth. It is (　　　) animal.
   ① a danger　　　② a dangerous　　　③ an endangered　　④ an in danger

2. Kana stopped buying sweets on her way home (　　　) save money.
   ① according to　　② due to　　　　③ in order to　　④ likely to

3. The company which started in Kyoto now has their offices (　　) the country.
   ① all over　　　　② between　　　③ during　　　　④ of all

4. Leaves of trees in the forest are turning red and yellow little (　　) little.
   ① by　　　　　　② of　　　　　③ on　　　　　④ to

5. She seems (　　) a boyfriend who is younger than her.
   ① have　　　　　② having　　　③ to have　　　④ to having

🎧 Listening　英文を聞いて理解しよう【知識・技能】【思考力・判断力・表現力】　共通テスト CD 28

Listen to the English and make the best choice to match the content. (4点)

　① The speaker and his sister have the same hobby of collecting panda items.

　② The speaker has a sister who collects panda character goods.

　③ The speaker's sister has seen more than thirty pandas.

💬 Interaction　英文を聞いて会話を続けよう【知識・技能】【思考力・判断力・表現力】　スピーキング・トレーナー CD 29

Listen to the English and respond to the last remark. (7点)

［メモ　　]

　アドバイス　実際に経験がなくても，会話を続けるために補足情報を加えよう。

💬 Production (Speak)　自分の考えを話して伝えよう【思考力・判断力・表現力】　スピーキング・トレーナー

Speak out your answer to the following question. (7点)

　Why are pandas so popular in Japan? Express your ideas.

　アドバイス　パンダのどんなところが好まれるのかを考え，知っている単語・表現を使って発信しよう。

Almost everyone / likes to see pandas. // But how about snakes? // Are they necessary / for our planet, / or not? //

① What do pandas, / **polar** bears / and gorillas / have in common? // Yes, / they are all animals. // In addition to being animals, / they are all endangered animals. // They might disappear / in the near future. // **Climate** change, / pollution / and human activities / are **threatening** their **survival**. //

② The International **Union** for the **Conservation** of Nature, / or IUCN, / is working / to save species / from **extinction**. // The IUCN Red List of Threatened Species / is used / to guide **decision-making** / for conservation action. // **According** to the list, / more than 13,000 animal species / are threatened / with extinction. //

③ We all care about / saving species / from extinction, / but a question might come to mind: / "Why should endangered species be protected?" // It is because all species play a role / in nature. // All species of life / on earth / are connected to each other / and are needed / for our planet / to stay healthy. // All animals are part of the global **ecosystem** / and are necessary / for the balance / of nature. // (172 words)

🔊 **音読しよう**　　　　　　　　　　　　　　　　　　　　スピーキング・トレーナー
Practice 1　スラッシュ位置で文を区切って読んでみよう ☐
Practice 2　イントネーションに注意して読んでみよう ☐
TRY!　　　　１分40秒以内に本文全体を音読しよう ☐

📖 **Reading**　本文の内容を読んで理解しよう【知識・技能】【思考力・判断力・表現力】　　共通テスト

Make the correct choice to complete each sentence or answer each question. (各4点)

1. Pandas, polar bears, and gorillas ☐ soon.
   ① are not at risk of extinction　　② have a similar appearance to each other
   ③ might no longer exist　　　　　　④ will not disappear at all

2. The IUCN Red List of Threatened Species is useful ☐.
   ① for judging how to plan conservation action
   ② for threatening endangered animals
   ③ to save animals which are threatening other species
   ④ to bring extinct animals back to life

3. Which of the following are true about endangered animals? (Choose two options. The order does not matter.) ☐ · ☐
   ① Over 10,000 of them have already become extinct.
   ② Some of them are protected by other species in nature.
   ③ They are important as a part of the ecosystem on earth.
   ④ Whether they will survive or not is influenced by human activities.

🔍 Vocabulary & Grammar　重要表現や文法事項について理解しよう【知識】　　英検® GTEC®

Make the correct choice to complete each sentence. (各2点)

1. Do any good ideas (　　　) mind about how to spend our next holiday?
   ① come to　　　② hit upon　　　③ make up　　　④ turn into

2. How long have your uncle and my father known (　　　)?
   ① both　　　② each other　　　③ one another　　　④ themselves

3. Two of my friends don't have much (　　　) common.
   ① for　　　② in　　　③ of　　　④ with

4. The king (　　　) a great role in English culture of the 17th century.
   ① became　　　② did　　　③ got　　　④ played

5. If it is clear tonight, many shooting stars will (　　　) in the west.
   ① be seen　　　② be seeing　　　③ see　　　④ seen

🎧 Listening　英文を聞いて理解しよう【知識・技能】【思考力・判断力・表現力】　共通テスト　CD 30

Listen to the English and make the best choice to match the content. (4点)

① The speaker advised his classmates to read books about endangered animals.

② The speaker was recommended to read about endangered animals.

③ The speaker's teacher read a book about endangered animals in class.

💬 Interaction　英文を聞いて会話を続けよう【知識・技能】【思考力・判断力・表現力】　スピーキング・トレーナー　CD 31

Listen to the English and respond to the last remark. (7点)

[メモ　　　　　　　　　　　　　　　　　　　　　　　　　　]

アドバイス　Which でたずねられているのでまず一つ選び，理由を述べよう。

✍ Production (Write)　自分の考えを書いて伝えよう【思考力・判断力・表現力】

Write your answer to the following question. (7点)

What role can humans play in the ecosystem? Write your ideas.

アドバイス　生態系を守るために，人間にしかできないことなどを考えてみよう。

37

④ There is an interesting survey. // One thousand people were asked / to **donate** some money / for endangered animals. // Almost all the people answered / that they would be interested in donating. // What kinds of animals / did they want to make a **donation** / to help? //

⑤ According to the survey, / 43 percent of the people / would donate / for the endangered animals / that they liked, / such as pandas and koalas. // On the other hand, / they would not donate / for animals / they didn't like, / such as snakes and **lizards**. // Most of them answered / that it was not fair / to help only attractive animals, though. //

⑥ It seems / that people like to protect animals / that they find attractive or cute. // Some companies **tend** to use such animals / in **advertisements** / to raise their sales. // It is true / that we are making efforts / to protect endangered animals. // However, / the animals that receive our **protection** / are often decided / by our personal **preferences**. // (151 words)

🔊 **音読しよう**   スピーキング・トレーナー

Practice 1   スラッシュ位置で文を区切って読んでみよう ☐
Practice 2   イントネーションに注意して読んでみよう ☐
TRY!   1分30秒以内に本文全体を音読しよう ☐

📖 **Reading**   本文の内容を読んで理解しよう【知識・技能】【思考力・判断力・表現力】   共通テスト

Make the correct choice to complete each sentence or answer each question. (各4点)

1. In the survey, ☐ answered that they would donate money for animals they liked.

   ① about four percent of the people

   ② almost all the people

   ③ more than half of the people

   ④ more than 400 people

2. The survey showed that many people ☐ animals such as snakes and lizards.

   ① agreed to help   ② didn't want to donate money for

   ③ tended to donate money for   ④ would make donations for

3. Which of the following is true about attractive or cute animals? ☐

   ① People sometimes decide to protect them in the zoo.

   ② People who like such animals always make a donation to help them.

   ③ They are often used by companies to draw customers' attention.

   ④ They receive humans' protection because they are useful for business activities.

🔍 Vocabulary & Grammar　重要表現や文法事項について理解しよう【知識】　　英検◎ GTEC◎

Make the correct choice to complete each sentence. (各2点)

1. Musicians asked people to (　　　) donations to rebuild the burned-down concert hall.
   ① achieve　　　② do　　　③ make　　　④ perform

2. Why don't we put (　　　) in our school newspaper next week?
   ① a development　② a government　③ an advertisement　④ an improvement

3. Personal (　　　) usually influence a person's thinking when deciding something.
   ① pleasures　　② politicians　　③ preferences　　④ products

4. Dogs (　　　) to get angry and bark at people they see for the first time.
   ① fail　　　② hope　　　③ mean　　　④ tend

5. Tom looks happy. It (　　　) his interview for the job went well.
   ① seem　　　② seemed that　③ seems that　④ seems to

🎧 Listening　英文を聞いて理解しよう【知識・技能】【思考力・判断力・表現力】　共通テスト CD 32

Listen to the English and make the best choice to match the content. (4点)

① The donation is not the first time for the speaker.

② The speaker has donated to help endangered animals only once.

③ The speaker made donations three times before this time.

💬 Interaction　英文を聞いて会話を続けよう【知識・技能】【思考力・判断力・表現力】　スピーキング・トレーナー CD 33

Listen to the English and respond to the last remark. (7点)

[メモ　　　　　　　　　　　　　　　　　　　　　　　　　　　　　　　　　　　　]

アドバイス　アイデアを求められているので, ask for donations on the Internet「インターネットで寄付を募る」
などの表現を用いてアドバイスしてあげよう。

✐ Production（Write）　自分の考えを書いて伝えよう【思考力・判断力・表現力】

Write your answer to the following question. (7点)

Do you want to make a donation? What will you donate to?

アドバイス　何に寄付したいか, またはなぜ寄付したくないかを明確に書こう。

----

7 Why do we think / that bears and pandas are cute? // First, / they have **human-like characteristics**. // Second, / they live in a family setting, / like bears and their babies. // Lastly, / we like larger animals. // Most smaller species, / such as insects, / tend to be **ignored**. // Some people say / that conservation today / is for "beautiful and useful species only." // Is it good for us / to protect only those species? //

8 We should not forget / that human beings are / one of the species / on earth. // Human society is / part of the global ecosystem. // We **gain** a lot of **benefits** / from the natural environment / and from the ecosystem. // They are called / ecosystem services. // They are the foundation / of all food and **agricultural** systems. //

9 Our lives are closely connected / to ecosystem services. // By protecting the environment and endangered species, / we help / not only the endangered animals / but also ourselves. // We have to think about this: / "How can we live / in **harmony** with nature / on a healthy planet?" // (159 words)

🔊 **音読しよう**　　　　　　　　　　　　　　　　　　　　スピーキング・トレーナー

Practice 1 　スラッシュ位置で文を区切って読んでみよう ☐
Practice 2 　イントネーションに注意して読んでみよう ☐
TRY! 　　　1分40秒以内に本文全体を音読しよう ☐

📖 **Reading**　本文の内容を読んで理解しよう【知識・技能】【思考力・判断力・表現力】　　共通テスト

Make the correct choice to complete each sentence or answer each question. (各4点)

1. Which is **not** true about bears and pandas? ☐

　① Most people tend to pay no attention to them.

　② They and their babies act like human parents and babies.

　③ They have similar characteristics to humans'.

　④ They seem to be more loved by humans than small insects.

2. If we protect endangered animals and the environment, it will help ☐ .

　① both endangered animals and human beings

　② either endangered animals or human beings

　③ neither endangered animals nor human beings

　④ only the endangered animals

3. One **fact** about the ecosystem is that ☐ .

　① ecosystem services are the source of agriculture

　② it is necessary not to ignore small species

　③ living in harmony with nature is important

　④ protecting only beautiful and useful species isn't good

🔎 Vocabulary & Grammar　重要表現や文法事項について理解しよう【知識】　　英検® GTEC®

Make the correct choice to complete each sentence. (各2点)

1. My brother is good at (　　　) studying but also sports.
   ① both　　　　② just as　　　　③ not only　　　　④ such as

2. The design of our new building is (　　　) the surrounding environment.
   ① according to　　② compared with　③ in harmony with　④ in relation to

3. The writer (　　　) a huge amount of money by the success of his first novel.
   ① gained　　　② grew　　　　③ recorded　　　④ produced

4. The dry weather seriously damaged (　　　) products in this area.
   ① agricultural　② environmental　③ global　　　④ human-like

5. How many students could (　　　) the problems within thirty minutes?
   ① be solved　　② have solving　　③ solve　　　④ solved

🎧 Listening　英文を聞いて理解しよう【知識・技能】【思考力・判断力・表現力】　共通テスト CD 34

Listen to the English and make the best choice to match the content. (4点)

① A report shows that the city got donations of $7,500 this year.

② The total amount of donations to the city increased from last year.

③ The total amount of this year's donations dropped by $7,500.

💬 Interaction　英文を聞いて会話を続けよう【知識・技能】【思考力・判断力・表現力】　スピーキング・トレーナー CD 35

Listen to the English and respond to the last remark. (7点)

［メモ　　　　　　　　　　　　　　　　　　　　　　　　　　　　　　　　］

アドバイス 相手の意見に同意できるかどうか，具体例や理由を挙げてみよう。

✎ Production (Write)　自分の考えを書いて伝えよう【思考力・判断力・表現力】

Write your answer to the following question. (7点)

Do you do something good for the environment? What do you do?

アドバイス 広範囲にわたるさまざまな活動が考えられる。自分の生活をよく思い返して書いてみよう。

You are looking / at a poster / about saving polar bears. //

Save the Polar Bear! //

　　Do you know / that polar bears spend / most of their lives / on the sea ice / of the **Arctic** Ocean? // They hunt for food / and raise their babies / on the ice. //

　　Due to climate change, / the sea ice is disappearing. // Because of this, / polar bears may become **extinct** / in the near future. // Their future is / in great danger. //

　　Help Polar Bears, / an NGO, / wants to protect / polar bears. // It has started a five-year **campaign** / to raise **awareness** / about their situation. // We ask for your support. // Any donations will be welcomed. // The money will **contribute** / to the following five areas: //

　　　　　1. Tracking polar bear mothers //

　　　　　2. **Monitoring** polar bear habitats //

　　　　　3. Mapping future polar bear habitats //

　　　　　4. Understanding climate change //

　　　　　5. **Preserving** the Arctic food **chain** //

　　You can help polar bears / and their polar home / by supporting Help Polar Bears. // We need your help. // If you are interested in this project, / please contact us / at

　　　　　https://www.helppolarbears.com. // (171 words)

◀)) 音読しよう　　　　　　　　　　　　　　　　スピーキング・トレーナー

Practice 1　スラッシュ位置で文を区切って読んでみよう☐

Practice 2　イントネーションに注意して読んでみよう☐

TRY!　　　　1分40秒以内に本文全体を音読しよう☐

📖 Reading　本文の内容を読んで理解しよう【知識・技能】【思考力・判断力・表現力】　　共通テスト

Make the correct choice to complete each sentence or answer each question. (各6点)

1. Which question about the polar bears can we answer from the poster? ☐

　① In how many years will polar bears become extinct?

　② What do they mainly eat for their food?

　③ When was the NGO, Help Polar Bears established?

　④ Why is their place to live decreasing?

2. The list of five statements in the poster shows us ☐.

　① a series of activities started five years ago

　② activities bringing money to Help Polar Bears

　③ the protection activities Help Polar Bears will support

　④ research to protect polar bears that has already been completed

🔊 イントネーションを理解して音読することができる。
📖 ホッキョクグマの保護に関する英文を読んで概要や要点を捉えることができる。
🔍 文脈を理解して適切な語句を用いて英文を完成することができる。　🎧 やや長めの英文を聞いて必要な情報を聞き取ることができる。

oals

🔍 Vocabulary & Grammar　重要表現や文法事項について理解しよう【知識】　英検® GTEC®

Make the correct choice to complete each sentence. (各2点)

1. A lot of small islands around the world are now in (　　　) of disappearing.
   ① afraid 　　　　② danger 　　　　③ front 　　　　④ progress

2. Doctors (　　　) awareness about having enough time to rest our eyes.
   ① notice 　　　　② offer 　　　　③ raise 　　　　④ warn

3. I hope this technology will contribute (　　　) the future of our country.
   ① on 　　　　② over 　　　　③ to 　　　　④ with

4. In the African ecosystem, the lion is at the top of the food (　　　).
   ① chain 　　　　② environment 　　　　③ group 　　　　④ system

5. (　　　) machine trouble, we couldn't buy tickets at the station.
   ① Because 　　　　② Due to 　　　　③ In order to 　　　　④ In spite of

6. All the air conditioners in the hall must be (　　　) off before you lock the entrance.
   ① to turn 　　　　② turn 　　　　③ turned 　　　　④ turning

7. Students can (　　　) the Wi-Fi network if they have their student ID and password.
   ① be using 　　　　② use 　　　　③ used 　　　　④ have used

8. It seems that people visiting Japan (　　　) in either Kyoto or Tokyo.
   ① stay 　　　　② stays 　　　　③ staying 　　　　④ to stay

🎧 Listening　英文を聞いて理解しよう【知識・技能】【思考力・判断力・表現力】　共通テスト CD 36

Listen to the English and make the best choice to match the content. (各4点)

1. How many sea turtles used to come up to the beach overnight in Michoacan?
   ① About 1,000. 　　　　② About 10,000.
   ③ About 20,000. 　　　　④ About 100,000.

2. What happened in 1978?
   ① Hunters took turtle eggs away from the beach.
   ② Many turtles were killed.
   ③ No turtles came to the beach.
   ④ WWF started a project in Mexico.

3. Which statement is true?
   ① Hunting against the law increased even after WWF began its project in Mexico.
   ② It took ten years for the WWF's project to have good results.
   ③ Students all over the world joined the turtle protection activities in Michoacan.
   ④ The Mexican government did nothing for sea turtles when they disappeared from the beach.

You want to go / to a *Curious George* **exhibit** / with your family. // You are looking at the exhibit website. //

Museum of Culture and Science. // Special Exhibit Events //

Let's Have Fun with *Curious George*! //

　Do you know / a cute little monkey / that always gets himself into trouble? // Yes, / it's George, / Curious George! // He is a good little monkey / and always very curious. //

　This **curiosity** leads him / to meet a man / with a yellow hat / and to travel / from Africa / to get a new home / in a zoo. // His curiosity gets George into trouble, / but it always helps him / out of it. //

　Let's experience the world / of *Curious George*! // In these exhibit events, / you can see buildings and places / from the *Curious George* books / and animations. // Experience a lot of new things / with curiosity. // These special events / will give you a wonderful experience / you won't forget! //

　Special appearance by George, / along with one of his stories, / at 10 a.m. and 1 p.m.! //

TICKETS //

・$21 for adults from 13 to 64 //

・$19 for adults 65 and over //

・$16 for children from 2 to 12 / (Children under 2 are free.) //

　A ticket **includes** / one special 45-minute **documentary** movie. //

TIME //

・Monday through Saturday / from 10 a.m. to 5 p.m. //

・Sunday / from noon to 6 p.m. //

PLACE //

　Museum of Culture and Science //

　401 North Second Street, Green Forest, FL 333XX //　(232 words)

🔊 **音読しよう**

Practice 1　スラッシュ位置で文を区切って読んでみよう ☐

Practice 2　イントネーションに注意して読んでみよう ☐

TRY!　　　　2分20秒以内に本文全体を音読しよう ☐

スピーキング・トレーナー

📖 **Reading**　本文の内容を読んで理解しよう【知識・技能】【思考力・判断力・表現力】　　共通テスト

Make the correct choice to complete each sentence or answer each question. (各6点)

1. Which of the following are true about the exhibit events? (Choose two options. The order does not matter.) ☐ ・ ☐

　① The events are held in the *Curious George* theme park.

　② The events provide visitors with the experience of animation production.

　③ Visitors can meet George himself there twice a day.

　④ Visitors can see a special movie at the event site.

2. A group of two 40-year-old adults with a 12-year-old child will cost ☐ to buy tickets for the events.

① $37.00　　　　② $58.00　　　　③ $61.00　　　　④ $63.00

🔍 Vocabulary & Grammar　重要表現や文法事項について理解しよう【知識】　英検® GTEC®

Make the correct choice to complete each sentence. (各2点)

1. My close friend has helped me (　　　　) of difficulties many times.
　① a lot　　　　② from　　　　③ one　　　　④ out

2. Bob's bad manners were always (　　　　) his family into trouble.
　① coming　　　② getting　　　③ making　　　④ taking

3. The photographer took about a hundred pictures to present at an (　　　) event.
　① exercise　　② exhibit　　　③ exist　　　④ experiment

4. Emi often tries very hot and spicy food out of (　　　).
　① charge　　　② condition　　③ control　　　④ curiosity

5. Even (　　　) professional soccer players sometimes lose a game with an own goal.
　① experience　② experienced　③ experiencing　④ experiences

🎧 Listening　英文を聞いて理解しよう【知識・技能】【思考力・判断力・表現力】　共通テスト CD 37

Listen to the English and make the best choice to match the content. (4点)

① The speaker has read a series of *Curious George* before.

② The speaker has seen *Curious George* in a movie theater.

③ The speaker knows some *Curious George* stories.

💬 Interaction　英文を聞いて会話を続けよう【知識・技能】【思考力・判断力・表現力】　スピーキング・トレーナー CD 38

Listen to the English and respond to the last remark. (7点)

[メモ　　]

アドバイス　相手と同じ意見のときは，also や，…, too などを使って伝えよう。

💬 Production (Speak)　自分の考えを話して伝えよう【思考力・判断力・表現力】　スピーキング・トレーナー

Speak out your answer to the following question. (7点)

Tell us one of your adventures that you remember most. How did you feel?

アドバイス　I remember the first time … 「はじめて…したときのことを覚えている」などの表現を使おう。

While millions of people know *Curious George*, / not many people know / about the careers / of his **creators**. // How did they create / one of the world's most famous monkeys? //

① Hans Augusto Rey was born / in Germany / in 1898 / to **Jewish** parents. // He grew up / a few blocks / from a zoo. // So he developed a **lifelong** love / for animals and drawing. // He met a young Jewish girl, / Margret, / at her sister's birthday party. // Later, / Margret left her hometown / to study art, / and they lost touch / for a while. //

② In 1935, / Hans and Margret met again / in Brazil. // Hans was doing some family business. // Margret was escaping the political climate / in Germany. // They decided to start working together. // They soon fell in love / and got **married** / in August. //

③ In 1936, / Hans and Margret traveled / to Paris, France. // They enjoyed Paris so much / that they decided to stay there. // Then Hans had a chance / to **publish** some of his animal drawings / in a French magazine. // His drawings became quite popular. //　That made the **publisher** decide to publish / Hans' first children's book, / *Raffy and the Nine Monkeys*, / in 1939. //　(184 words)

🔊 **音読しよう**　　　　　　　　　　　　　　スピーキング・トレーナー
Practice 1　スラッシュ位置で文を区切って読んでみよう □
Practice 2　イントネーションに注意して読んでみよう □
TRY!　　　　１分50秒以内に本文全体を音読しよう □

📖 **Reading**　本文の内容を読んで理解しよう【知識・技能】【思考力・判断力・表現力】　　共通テスト

Make the correct choice to complete each sentence or answer each question. (各4点)

1. Hans Augusto Rey was born ☐.

　① at the end of the nineteenth century

　② in Brazil

　③ in the late eighteenth century

　④ to artist parents

2. Which of the following is **not** true about Hans in his younger days? ☐

　① He left his hometown earlier than Margret.

　② He used to have a lot of chances to see animals.

　③ He was born and raised in a Jewish family.

　④ He went to Margret's sister's birthday party.

3. Hans married Margret when they were in ☐.

　① Brazil　　　　② Germany　　　　③ France　　　　④ their hometown

🔍 Vocabulary & Grammar 　重要表現や文法事項について理解しよう【知識】　　英検® GTEC®

Make the correct choice to complete each sentence. （各2点）

1. My friend left our town ten years ago. I've lost (　　　　) with him since then.
   ① call 　　　　　② hearing 　　　　③ meetings 　　　　④ touch

2. John (　　　　) love with Yoko after they met at the art gallery.
   ① fell in 　　　　② felt for 　　　　③ filled in 　　　　④ found out

3. My grandmother was in the hospital for a (　　　　) last month.
   ① during 　　　　② long 　　　　　③ term 　　　　　④ while

4. (　　　　) copies of the book by the author have been sold in Japan.
   ① Million 　　　　② Million of 　　　③ Millions 　　　④ Millions of

5. Did you hear Shota (　　　　) German?
   ① speak 　　　　　② speaks 　　　　③ spoke 　　　　④ to speak

🎧 Listening 　英文を聞いて理解しよう【知識・技能】【思考力・判断力・表現力】　共通テスト　CD 39

Listen to the English and make the best choice to match the content. （4点）

① It has been 32 years since the speaker got married.

② The speaker and his wife have been married for twenty years.

③ The speaker is 42 years old now.

💬 Interaction 　英文を聞いて会話を続けよう【知識・技能】【思考力・判断力・表現力】　スピーキング・トレーナー　CD 40

Listen to the English and respond to the last remark. （7点）

［メモ　　　　　　　　　　　　　　　　　　　　　　　　　　　　　　　　　　　　　　］

　アドバイス　最初のあなたの発言についてもよく聞き取ろう。

✐ Production（Write） 　自分の考えを書いて伝えよう【思考力・判断力・表現力】

Write your answer to the following question. （7点）

Do you want to marry in the future? If so, by what age do you want to marry?

　アドバイス　「いいえ」の場合は，そう考える理由をそえよう。

4　Only a few months / after Hans' book was published, / World War II broke out / in 1939. // Since they were German **Jews** / in Paris, / Hans and Margret Rey felt / they would be in danger. // In June 1940, / the **Nazi army** / was rapidly **approaching** Paris. //

5　There were no more trains, / and the Reys didn't own a car. // They had to find a way / to get away / from Paris. // Hans hurried over / to a bicycle shop, / but there were no bicycles / for them. // Only **spare** parts were **available**. // That night, / Hans put the parts together / to make two bicycles. //

6　Early in the morning / of June 12, / 1940, / the Reys set off / on their bicycles. // They took very little with them: / warm clothes, / some food / and some **unpublished manuscripts** / of children's books. // They included one special book, / *Fifi: The Adventures of a Monkey*. // It was just 48 hours / before the Nazi army **marched** / into Paris. // They were finally / among the millions of **refugees** / trying to run away / to the south. // (166 words)

🔊 **音読しよう**　　　　　　　　　　　　　　　　　　スピーキング・トレーナー
Practice 1　スラッシュ位置で文を区切って読んでみよう ☐
Practice 2　イントネーションに注意して読んでみよう ☐
TRY!　　　　1分40秒以内に本文全体を音読しよう ☐

📖 **Reading**　本文の内容を読んで理解しよう【知識・技能】【思考力・判断力・表現力】　　共通テスト

Make the correct choice to complete each sentence or answer each question. (各4点)

1. Hans wanted [＿＿＿], but he couldn't.
   ① to buy two bicycles
   ② to get away from Paris
   ③ to get some bicycle parts
   ④ to go to Paris

2. Which of the following events did **not** take place in June 1940? [＿＿＿]
   ① Hans' first book was released into the market.
   ② Hans went to the bicycle shop to get bicycles.
   ③ The Nazi army from Germany reached Paris.
   ④ The Reys left their home for the south of France.

3. The Nazi army marched into Paris on [＿＿＿], 1940.
   ① June 10
   ② June 12
   ③ June 14
   ④ June 16

🔍 Vocabulary & Grammar　重要表現や文法事項について理解しよう【知識】　　英検® GTEC®

Make the correct choice to complete each sentence. (各2点)

1. The Japanese research team has (　　　　) for London by plane.

　① got along　　　　② put off　　　　③ set off　　　　④ taken over

2. Only (　　　) minutes later, my sister came home from work.

　① a few　　　　② a fewer　　　　③ few　　　　④ the few

3. We have to put those hundreds of pieces (　　　) to complete the puzzle.

　① away　　　　② on　　　　③ together　　　　④ with

4. If a forest fire (　　　) out in the mountains, that will kill a lot of animals there.

　① breaks　　　　② goes　　　　③ happens　　　　④ turns

5. The coming typhoon will make us (　　　) the plan for our trip.

　① cancel　　　　② canceled　　　　③ canceling　　　　④ to cancel

🎧 Listening　英文を聞いて理解しよう【知識・技能】【思考力・判断力・表現力】　　共通テスト　CD 41

Listen to the English and make the best choice to match the content. (4点)

　① The speaker's grandfather couldn't go to university because of the war.

　② The speaker's grandfather entered university before World War II began.

　③ World War II broke out after the speaker's grandfather graduated from university.

💬 Interaction　英文を聞いて会話を続けよう【知識・技能】【思考力・判断力・表現力】　スピーキング・トレーナー　CD 42

Listen to the English and respond to the last remark. (7点)

　［メモ　　　　　　　　　　　　　　　　　　　　　　　　　　　　　　　　　　　　　　］

　アドバイス　何が必要になるか想像し、その理由などを答えよう。

✐ Production（Write）　自分の考えを書いて伝えよう【思考力・判断力・表現力】

Write your answer to the following question. (7点)

　When the Reys left Paris, why did they take their unpublished manuscripts of children's books with them? Imagine and write your ideas.

　アドバイス　レイ夫妻になったつもりで考えてみよう。emotional support「心の支え」　source of income「収入源」

49

⑦　Hans and Margret slept / in **barns** / and on floors / of restaurants / on the way south. // Finally, / they came across running trains. // This was their chance / to get out of France. // However, / a **checkpoint** officer became **suspicious** / of their German **accents**. // When he **searched** their bags / and found the manuscript of *Fifi*, / he was sure / that they were not German spies. // Thanks to their cute little monkey, / the Reys passed through Spain / and made it out of Europe / to Brazil / by ship. // After reaching Brazil, / they continued on / to New York. //

⑧　In October 1940, / Hans and Margret arrived safely / in America. // One year later, / *Fifi: The Adventures of a Monkey* / was published / in America / under the new name: / *Curious George*. //

⑨　Think of all the smiles / around the world / that have been made / by one **mischievous** little monkey! // *Curious George* / seems to **reflect** / what his creators experienced / while they were escaping the Nazis. // Who knew / such a **historic** adventure / was behind a warm character / of **innocent mischief**? // (165 words)

🔊 **音読しよう**　　　　　　　　　　　　　　　　　スピーキング・トレーナー

Practice 1　スラッシュ位置で文を区切って読んでみよう ☐
Practice 2　イントネーションに注意して読んでみよう ☐
TRY!　　　1分40秒以内に本文全体を音読しよう ☐

📖 **Reading**　本文の内容を読んで理解しよう【知識・技能】【思考力・判断力・表現力】　　共通テスト

Make the correct choice to complete each sentence or answer each question. (各4点)

1. Hans and Margret tried to enter ☐ .

　① France from Brazil

　② Spain from Brazil

　③ Spain from France

　④ New York from Germany

2. The checkpoint officer probably told Hans and Margret ☐ .

　① to become suspicious of his German accent

　② to draw some pictures of monkeys

　③ to get out of Spain

　④ to show him their bags

3. Which of the following is true about *Curious George*? ☐

　① Hans had a monkey which influenced the story.

　② It went on sale before the Reys arrived in New York.

　③ Its title was changed from *Fifi: The Adventures of a Monkey*.

　④ The book was published in October 1940.

🔍 Vocabulary & Grammar　重要表現や文法事項について理解しよう【知識】　　英検® GTEC®

Make the correct choice to complete each sentence. (各2点)

1. Can you stop by a supermarket (　　　　) the way home and get an apple?

　① before　　　　② in　　　　③ on　　　　④ while

2. She became (　　　) of his behavior and called the police.

　① historic　　　② innocent　　　③ mischievous　　　④ suspicious

3. Our new price will (　　　) the rise in the material cost in recent years.

　① direct　　　② effect　　　③ reflect　　　④ result

4. Can you believe I came (　　　) a wild monkey on the university campus?

　① across　　　② around　　　③ away　　　④ together

5. Excuse me, but I haven't received (　　　) I ordered from your store two weeks ago.

　① what　　　② which　　　③ who　　　④ whose

🎧 Listening　英文を聞いて理解しよう【知識・技能】【思考力・判断力・表現力】　　共通テスト CD 43

Listen to the English and make the best choice to match the content. (4点)

　① The speaker didn't stop by Florence and went to Venice.

　② The speaker stayed in Rome, Florence and Venice.

　③ The speaker went to Rome after leaving Venice.

💬 Interaction　英文を聞いて会話を続けよう【知識・技能】【思考力・判断力・表現力】　スピーキング・トレーナー　CD 44

Listen to the English and respond to the last remark. (7点)

　[メモ　　　　　　　　　　　　　　　　　　　　　　　　　　　　　　　　　　　　]

　アドバイス　単に質問に答えるだけでなく，あらすじやそれを選んだ理由も述べよう。

✐ Production (Write)　自分の考えを書いて伝えよう【思考力・判断力・表現力】

Write your answer to the following question. (7点)

　Why did the manuscript of *Fifi* make the check point officer think the Reys were not German spies? Imagine and write your ideas.

　アドバイス　検問官はスパイにどのような印象を持っていたのか想像してみよう。cannot be ... 「…のはずがない」

In 2017, / the *Curious George* documentary / *MONKEY BUSINESS* / was released / by a film **director**, / Ema Ryan Yamazaki. // You are listening to an interview / with her. //

Q1) What made you decide / to become a film director? //

　When I was in high school, / I began telling stories / with a camera. // I realized / I had a **passion** / for sharing / what I found interesting / with others. // So I decided / to study **filmmaking** / in college, / and it has led me / to this career. //

Q2) Why did you choose / *Curious George* / and its creators / as the theme / of your work? //

　I happened to learn / about the creators / of *Curious George* / from a friend. // I loved *Curious George*, / but I didn't know anything / about his creators / before then. // I was **inspired** / when I knew / that they experienced hardships / but left behind wonderful stories / and a cute character. // I thought / that their story should be shared / with the world. //

Q3) Please give your message / to high school students. //

　I was lucky / to find my passion / in high school, / and now / I have a career / in doing what I enjoy the most. // I learned a lot / from the creators / of *Curious George*. // I hope / your curiosity will drive you / to discover / what you like / and to see life / as an adventure! //　(180 words)

🔊 **音読しよう**　　　　　　　　　　　　　　　　　　　　スピーキング・トレーナー

Practice 1　スラッシュ位置で文を区切って読んでみよう☐
Practice 2　イントネーションに注意して読んでみよう☐
TRY!　　　　1分50秒以内に本文全体を音読しよう☐

📖 **Reading**　本文の内容を読んで理解しよう【知識・技能】【思考力・判断力・表現力】　　　共通テスト

Make the correct choice to complete each sentence. (各6点)

1. Ema felt she should share the Reys' story with others ☐ .
   ① after she learned about it　　　② when she was a high school student
   ③ when she was interviewed　　　④ when she was working on it

2. One **fact** from the interview is that ☐ .
   ① curiosity will drive people to discover what they like
   ② Ema learned about the Reys from her friend
   ③ high school students should see life as an adventure
   ④ the stories of the creators of *Curious George* should be shared with the world

🔍 Vocabulary & Grammar 重要表現や文法事項について理解しよう【知識】 英検◦ GTEC◦

Make the correct choice to complete each sentence. (各2点)

1. Why don't you share your opinions (　　　) us?
   ① between　　　② for　　　③ to　　　④ with

2. I (　　　) to find my lost key under the cushion when I removed it.
   ① appeared　　　② failed　　　③ had　　　④ happened

3. It took about a month for my pet dog to (　　　) me as his master.
   ① look at　　　② know　　　③ see　　　④ watch

4. The (　　　) of the public library always managed his staff with respect.
   ① captain　　　② director　　　③ professor　　　④ president

5. When Mari goes to school, she sometimes leaves her smartphone (　　　).
   ① after　　　② back　　　③ before　　　④ behind

6. All of these six routes will (　　　) you to the city center.
   ① arrive　　　② go　　　③ lead　　　④ leave

7. Our tour conductor (　　　) us wait in front of the ticket counter.
   ① allowed　　　② got　　　③ had　　　④ kept

8. (　　　) Mr. White told us to do was to stay healthy during the vacation.
   ① It　　　② It was　　　③ That　　　④ What

🎧 Listening 英文を聞いて理解しよう【知識・技能】【思考力・判断力・表現力】 共通テスト CD ◎ 45

Listen to the English and make the best choice to match the content. (各4点)

1. When did J.K. Rowling get the idea for *Harry Potter*?
   ① After she got off a train.　　　② In her teens.
   ③ On her way home.　　　④ When she was six.

2. What happened while she wrote the story of the first volume of *Harry Potter*?
   ① Her love of writing often disappeared.
   ② Her mother became a single mother.
   ③ She broke up with her lover.
   ④ She started to live without her husband.

3. Which statement is true about the first volume of *Harry Potter*?
   ① It didn't sell as well as the following volumes of *Harry Potter*.
   ② It was not on sale soon after she completed the story.
   ③ It was not sold in the U.S.
   ④ It was written in a lot of languages by J.K. Rowling.

You are listening to a poster presentation / about "The Poorest President in the World." //

The Poorest President in the World //

Jose Mujica //

Born: May 20, 1935 // Family: wife, pets and other animals //

His Life — Very Unusual for a President! //

Mr. Mujica … //

· leads a very simple life / near Montevideo, / the capital of **Uruguay**. //

· loves taking care of animals and plants / on his farm. //

· likes reading very much / and gives most of his books / to schools later. //

· never wears expensive clothes / and never wears a tie, / even with his suit. //

· lived on a low **salary** / even when he was the president. //

· didn't live in the president's **official residence**, / and didn't use the president's official car / or the president's official plane. //

Mr. Mujica was born / into a poor family / in Uruguay / in 1935. // His father died / when he was seven, / and his mother supported the family. // When he was a university student, / the **economy** of his country / was in a bad condition / and the difference of quality of life / between the rich and the poor / was large. // He decided to do something / to help his country. // After he graduated from university, / he **protested** against the government. // He was **arrested** several times, / but he never lost hope. // He was finally released / in 1985 / and became a politician / ten years later. // In 2009, / he was **elected** president / of Uruguay. //

(232 words)

🔊 音読しよう

スピーキング・トレーナー

Practice 1　スラッシュ位置で文を区切って読んでみよう ☐
Practice 2　イントネーションに注意して読んでみよう ☐
TRY!　　　 2分20秒以内に本文全体を音読しよう ☐

📖 **Reading**　本文の内容を読んで理解しよう【知識・技能】【思考力・判断力・表現力】　　共通テスト

Make the correct choice to complete each sentence or answer each question. (各6点)

1. Which of the following is **not** true about Mr. Mujica? ☐

① He didn't mind giving books for free.

② He put on a necktie only when he wore suits.

③ He used neither the president's official car nor plane.

④ His income wasn't so good while he was president.

- イントネーションを理解して音読することができる。
- 文脈を理解して適切な語句を用いて英文を完成することができる。
- ペットについて簡単な語句を用いて考えを表現することができる。
- ホセ・ムヒカに関する英文を読んで概要や要点を捉えることができる。
- 平易な英語で話される短い英文を聞いて必要な情報を聞き取ることができる。
- 社会問題について簡単な語句を用いて考えを表現することができる。

oals

2. In 1995, Mr. Mujica ⬚ .

  ① became the president of his country

  ② began his career as a politician

  ③ was in his 10th year after he became a politician

  ④ was released from prison and got his freedom

🔍 Vocabulary & Grammar　重要表現や文法事項について理解しよう【知識】　英検® GTEC®

Make the correct choice to complete each sentence.（各2点）

1. You can get our original free desktop wallpaper from our (　　) website.

  ① company　　　② official　　　③ personal　　　④ publish

2. I had to (　　) very little money for a while after I lost my wallet.

  ① live for　　　② live on　　　③ live without　　　④ pay for

3. I'm sorry you caught a cold. Please take (　　) yourself.

  ① a look at　　　② care of　　　③ it easy　　　④ part in

4. Mr. Campbell (　　) a very active life in Australia.

  ① goes on　　　② keeps　　　③ leads　　　④ stays

5. (　　) the shop is going to have a sale for clothes next week.

  ① It seeming that　　② It seems that　　③ It seems to　　④ That seems to

🎧 Listening　英文を聞いて理解しよう【知識・技能】【思考力・判断力・表現力】　共通テスト　CD 46

Listen to the English and make the best choice to match the content.（4点）

  ① The teacher doesn't wear a suit even when he talks with his students' parents.

  ② The teacher doesn't wear a suit unless he meets his students' parents.

  ③ The teacher never wears a suit.

💬 Interaction　英文を聞いて会話を続けよう【知識・技能】【思考力・判断力・表現力】　スピーキング・トレーナー　CD 47

Listen to the English and respond to the last remark.（7点）

[メモ　　　　　　　　　　　　　　　　　　　　　　　　　　　　　　　　　　　]

　アドバイス　今ではなく，「大人になってから」のことを想像して答えよう。

💬 Production (Speak)　自分の考えを話して伝えよう【思考力・判断力・表現力】　スピーキング・トレーナー

Speak out your answer to the following question.（7点）

  If you become the president of your country, what problem do you want to solve?

　アドバイス　自分が国のトップになったつもりで考えよう。

Why did Jose Mujica come to be called / "the poorest president in the world"? // What does he think / about that? //

① **Laundry hangs** / outside the house. // Water comes / from a well / in a yard / full of tall grass. // Only two police officers / and a dog / keep watch outside. // This is the house / of a former president / of Uruguay, / Jose Mujica. // It is on a farm / outside the capital, / Montevideo. //

② Mujica went to work / from this residence / even during his service / as president. // He didn't want to move / to the official residence / when he was elected / in 2009. // He donated / most of his salary / to charities. // His **monthly income** was / about 1,000 dollars. // It was very low / for a leader / of a country, / so he was seen / as "the poorest president in the world." //

③ "I'm called the poorest president, / but I don't feel poor," / Mujica says. // "A president is a **high-level** official / who is elected / to carry out his or her **duty**. // A president is not a king, / not a god. // A president is a **civil servant**. // The ideal way of living / is to live / like the **majority** of people." //　(188 words)

🔊 **音読しよう**

スピーキング・トレーナー

Practice 1　スラッシュ位置で文を区切って読んでみよう ☐
Practice 2　イントネーションに注意して読んでみよう ☐
TRY!　　　　1分50秒以内に本文全体を音読しよう ☐

📖 **Reading**　本文の内容を読んで理解しよう【知識・技能】【思考力・判断力・表現力】　　共通テスト

Make the correct choice to complete each sentence or answer each question. (各4点)

1. Which of the following are true about Mujica's private life? (Choose two options. The order does not matter.) ☐ ・ ☐

    ① He has to go to the well far from his house to get drinking water.

    ② He lives in a house with a natural garden.

    ③ His family is kept safe thanks to police officers.

    ④ There are large glass windows on the wall of his house.

2. When Mujica was a president, he ☐ .

    ① didn't mind giving money to help people

    ② earned too little to donate money to charity

    ③ moved to the official residence outside Montevideo

    ④ was often seen as the poorest citizen

3. Mujica doesn't think he ⬚.

① lives the ideal way   ② needs more money

③ wants to be poor   ④ was called the poorest president

🔍 Vocabulary & Grammar　重要表現や文法事項について理解しよう【知識】　英検® GTEC®

Make the correct choice to complete each sentence.（各2点）

1. The (　　　) of students at this university come to campus by train or bus.

　① large　　　② major　　　③ majority　　　④ number

2. Where is this noise (　　　)?

　① bring to　　② coming from　　③ going to　　④ staying in

3. The entrance closes at 10 p.m., and some security staff began to (　　) watch.

　① keep　　　② protect　　　③ stay　　　④ turn

4. Let's think about the way to (　　　) our tasks more efficiently.

　① bring on　　② carry out　　③ lift up　　④ take place

5. (　　　) you need is enough rest.

　① It　　　② That　　　③ What　　　④ Which

🎧 Listening　英文を聞いて理解しよう【知識・技能】【思考力・判断力・表現力】　共通テスト　CD 48

Listen to the English and make the best choice to match the content.（4点）

　① Almost all the citizens of the country voted for him in the presidential election.

　② Many people in the country were happy to choose him as president.

　③ More than half the citizens were satisfied with the new mayor.

💬 Interaction　英文を聞いて会話を続けよう【知識・技能】【思考力・判断力・表現力】　スピーキング・トレーナー　CD 49

Listen to the English and respond to the last remark.（7点）

　［メモ　　］

　アドバイス　あなたが忙しいときはどんなことをしたいと思うか，想像しよう。どうしてそう思うか相手に伝わる
　　　　　ように理由なども加えよう。

✍ Production（Write）　自分の考えを書いて伝えよう【思考力・判断力・表現力】

Write your answer to the following question.（7点）

　Which would you choose, a rich but busy life or a poor but comfortable life?　Why?

　アドバイス　なぜその生活を選んだか，相手に納得してもらえるような理由を考えよう。

④ In April 2016, / Mujica was invited / to Japan / for the first time / because a Japanese publisher had just begun / to sell the book, / *The Poorest President in the World*. // He gave a speech / to young Japanese people / at Tokyo University of Foreign Studies. // In his **casual** clothes, / he didn't look like someone / who had been a president / of a country / for five years. //

⑤ Mujica **delivered** a message / about happiness and **poverty**. // In his address, / he **stressed** the importance / of love / for our happiness. // He said / that it is the most important thing / in the world / for us people. // "If people cannot share / the feeling of love / with their family, / friends / or neighbors, / they are poor. // The greatest poverty / in this world / is **loneliness**." //

⑥ According to Mujica, / poverty is not about what we have / or how much we have, / not a matter of **wealth**. // "I'm not the poorest president. // I can live well / with what I have. // The poorest person is the one / who needs a lot to live." //

(168 words)

🔊 **音読しよう**

Practice 1　スラッシュ位置で文を区切って読んでみよう☐
Practice 2　イントネーションに注意して読んでみよう☐
TRY!　　　1分40秒以内に本文全体を音読しよう☐

スピーキング・トレーナー

📖 **Reading**　本文の内容を読んで理解しよう【知識・技能】【思考力・判断力・表現力】　共通テスト

Make the correct choice to complete each sentence or answer each question. (各4点)

1. The book, *The Poorest President in the World,* was published ☐.

   ① after Mujica came to Japan

   ② before Mujica came to Japan

   ③ when Mujica gave a speech in Tokyo

   ④ while Mujica was the president of Uruguay

2. Mujica ☐ when he gave a speech.

   ① didn't wear a suit or tie　　　② looked like a real president

   ③ looked so rich　　　　　　　④ talked about casual clothes

3. Which of the following is most likely to be Mujica's motto? ☐

   ① "Happiness will come to one who loves people around him or her."

   ② "The happiest person doesn't mind being lonely."

   ③ "The poorest person is the one who lives a life full of love."

   ④ "Those who know how much they need are poor."

🔍 Vocabulary & Grammar　重要表現や文法事項について理解しよう【知識】　　英検® GTEC®

Make the correct choice to complete each sentence. (各2点)

1. The owner got great (　　　) in a few years through his business.
   ① prize　　　　② sunshine　　　　③ treasure　　　　④ wealth

2. I visited New York (　　　) the first time last year.
   ① for　　　　② in　　　　③ on　　　　④ with

3. She looked nervous. She was asked to (　　　) a speech at an event.
   ① give　　　　② do　　　　③ present　　　　④ show

4. (　　　) is one of the social problems we have to solve in the world.
   ① Curiosity　　　　② Poverty　　　　③ Reality　　　　④ Variety

5. My grandmother (　　　) a diary until she passed away in 2018.
   ① had kept　　　　② has kept　　　　③ have kept　　　　④ was keeping

🎧 Listening　英文を聞いて理解しよう【知識・技能】【思考力・判断力・表現力】　共通テスト CD 50

Listen to the English and make the best choice to match the content. (4点)

① The speaker has invited a person to give a speech.

② The speaker is going to give a speech.

③ The speaker will not attend the event.

💬 Interaction　英文を聞いて会話を続けよう【知識・技能】【思考力・判断力・表現力】　スピーキング・トレーナー CD 51

Listen to the English and respond to the last remark. (7点)

［メモ　　　　　　　　　　　　　　　　　　　　　　　　　　　　　　　　］

アドバイス　疑問文ではないが，相手の状況を理解し，どんな言葉をかければよいか考えよう。

✏️ Production (Write)　自分の考えを書いて伝えよう【思考力・判断力・表現力】

Write your answer to the following question. (7点)

Mujica said that the person who needs a lot to live is poor. Do you agree with that?

アドバイス　なぜ賛成［反対］か理由を述べよう。この文より前のムヒカの言葉，考えがヒントになるだろう。

7 Mujica thinks highly of **educating** young people. // As a politician, / he believes / that good education has the power / to change the world / in the future. // Every time / he visits a foreign country, / he gives a speech / to young people, / especially university students. //

8 In Tokyo, / Mujica said / that Japanese students should ask themselves / what happiness is / and what poverty is. // He told them / that wealth is not what matters most, / and that we should not spend / all of our time / worrying about **material** things. // He stressed / that life is not only about earning money. // His words greatly impressed / the young people / of Japan. //

9 Japan is a highly developed country, / and we are surrounded / by various kinds of **consumer** goods / and **high-tech** products. // Japan has **pursued economic growth** / for decades, / but many people say / they are not **satisfied**. // A survey shows / that people's sense of happiness / in Japan / is not very high / among the **industrialized** nations. // Jose Mujica's message / teaches us / very important things / about how we should think / about happiness. // (169 words)

🔊 **音読しよう**　　　　　　　　　　　　　　　　　　　　　　スピーキング・トレーナー
Practice 1　スラッシュ位置で文を区切って読んでみよう ☐
Practice 2　イントネーションに注意して読んでみよう ☐
TRY!　　　　1分40秒以内に本文全体を音読しよう ☐

📖 **Reading**　本文の内容を読んで理解しよう【知識・技能】【思考力・判断力・表現力】　　共通テスト

Make the correct choice to complete each sentence. (各4点)

1. Whenever he went overseas, Mujica ☐ there.

　① discussed education with politicians

　② had a chance to deliver his message to young people

　③ listened to the speeches of university students

　④ studied at a university

2. One **fact** about Mujica's message to Japanese young people is that ☐ .

　① many Japanese young people were moved by it

　② there are a lot of things in life besides making money

　③ wealth is not everything we need

　④ we should not worry about material things

3. One **opinion** about Japanese people is that ▢.

　① many of them are not satisfied with their life

　② Mujica's message is important for them to think about happiness

　③ their sense of happiness is lower

　④ they can easily find high-tech products around them

🔍 **Vocabulary & Grammar**　重要表現や文法事項について理解しよう【知識】　　英検® GTEC®

Make the correct choice to complete each sentence. (各2点)

1. The painter has created excellent works for (　　　).

　① decades　　　② decides　　　③ demands　　　④ diseases

2. Baseball fans (　　　) his skills of throwing the ball correctly.

　① highly of think　② highly think of　③ think highly of　④ think of highly

3. Our teachers post pictures on the school's website (　　　) time it has an event.

　① all　　　② every　　　③ some　　　④ when

4. He plans to move to the U.S. to (　　　) his dream to be a movie director.

　① continue　　② find　　　③ pursue　　　④ spread

5. I can't remember when (　　　) this pair of shoes.

　① did I buy　　② I bought　　③ I buying　　④ was I buying

🎧 **Listening**　英文を聞いて理解しよう【知識・技能】【思考力・判断力・表現力】　共通テスト CD 52

Listen to the English and make the best choice to match the content. (4点)

　① The speaker and her mother graduated from the same high school.

　② The speaker wants to go to the same university her mother graduated from.

　③ The speaker's mother went to the university the speaker goes to now.

💬 **Interaction**　英文を聞いて会話を続けよう【知識・技能】【思考力・判断力・表現力】　スピーキング・トレーナー CD 53

Listen to the English and respond to the last remark. (7点)

　[メモ　　　　　　　　　　　　　　　　　　　　　　　　　　　　　　]

　アドバイス　日常生活をよく思い返し,小さな幸せをひとつ見つけよう。

✏️ **Production（Write）**　自分の考えを書いて伝えよう【思考力・判断力・表現力】

Write your answer to the following question. (7点)

　What is the most important thing to you?

　アドバイス　選ぶものは物でも人でもよい。そう考える理由も考えてみよう。

After a university student listened to Mujica's speech, / he studied happiness / in various countries. // He made a report / to present in class. //

The **United Nations** / has published the World Happiness Report / every year / since 2012. // It is a survey / of the state / of global happiness, / and it ranks more than 150 countries / by their happiness levels. //

The state of happiness / in this report / comes from several kinds of **data**: / GDP **per** person, / healthy life **expectancy**, / and data / from 1,000 people / in each country / about happiness. // The questions ask people / to **rate** several parts / of their lives / by using numbers / from zero to ten. // Zero is the worst possible life / and ten is the best. // The following are the results / from some of the past few years. //

Three or four of the top five / each year / are Northern European countries. // They are thought / to be the most highly developed **welfare** countries / in the world. // Most people in these countries feel / that they are healthy, / comfortable / and happy. //

On the other hand, / Japan ranks much lower / **regarding** happiness. // It is the lowest / among the G7 nations. // Japan is one of the leading countries / in some ways, / for example, / in economy and technology. // However, / Japanese people do not rank very high / for feeling healthy, / comfortable / and happy. // What is important / for us / to feel happy? // (222 words)

◀)) 音読しよう

スピーキング・トレーナー

Practice 1 スラッシュ位置で文を区切って読んでみよう□
Practice 2 イントネーションに注意して読んでみよう□
TRY!   2分10秒以内に本文全体を音読しよう□

📖 **Reading** 本文の内容を読んで理解しよう【知識・技能】【思考力・判断力・表現力】   共通テスト

Make the correct choice to complete each sentence or answer each question. (各6点)

1. [   ] people all over the world answer the questions about their level of happiness every year.

   ① About 1,000   ② More than 150
   ③ More than 150,000   ④ Over 1,500,000

2. Which of the following is true about the World Happiness Report? [   ]

   ① Japan sometimes doesn't appear in the report.
   ② Northern European countries have been ranked very high.
   ③ The average life expectancy of citizens is used as data for the report.
   ④ The United Nations has published over thirty World Happiness Reports.

🔍 Vocabulary & Grammar 重要表現や文法事項について理解しよう【知識】   英検® GTEC®

Make the correct choice to complete each sentence. (各2点)

1. The price of this T-shirt is the lowest, but (   ) the quality, it's not the best.
   ① reflecting   ② regarding   ③ researching   ④ resulting

2. Many people (   ) him highly as a pianist.
   ① ate   ② date   ③ late   ④ rate

3. We express the speed with the distance which an object travels (   ) hour.
   ① between   ② by   ③ over   ④ per

4. The city spends enough money every year to maintain good (   ) services.
   ① wallet   ② wealth   ③ welfare   ④ welcome

5. Judges will (   ) the twelve dancers by their technical skills and power of expression.
   ① decide   ② rank   ③ watch   ④ win

6. When he arrived at the station, the train (   ) already left for London.
   ① had   ② has   ③ having   ④ was

7. Maki said that she (   ) to England three times.
   ① has visited   ② had been
   ③ had been traveling   ④ had went

8. Do you know how many fish (   ) in the sea?
   ① did he catch   ② has he catching   ③ have caught   ④ he caught

🎧 Listening 英文を聞いて理解しよう【知識・技能】【思考力・判断力・表現力】   共通テスト CD 54

Listen to the English and make the best choice to match the content. (各4点)

1. Why did the Gross National Happiness begin in Bhutan?
   ① Because a king appeared in Bhutan for the first time.
   ② Because Bhutan was called the happiest country in the world.
   ③ Because it was proposed by the king.
   ④ Because the Bhutanese king did a survey.

2. Which of the following is true about the GNH?
   ① About 10,000 people answer the survey.
   ② It is done every year.
   ③ It shows the percentage of people who own a car.
   ④ The king has an interview with citizens.

3. How many people in Bhutan seem to have their own car?
   ① About one in seventy people.   ② About one-seventh of the citizens.
   ③ About seven thousand people.   ④ About ten thousand citizens.

You want to learn / something about Seattle. // You have found / the following **blog** post. //

Hello from Seattle! // Oct 5, 2020 //

I stopped for coffee / at a café. // This was an **iced** coffee / served there. // Look at the **straw**. // It was made of paper, / not plastic! //

At first, / I was a **bit** afraid / that it would soon get wet and soft, / but there was no problem / at all. // The paper straw / was actually very strong. // I felt no difference / from a plastic straw! //

Why didn't the café use / plastic straws? // Seattle hopes to reduce / plastic waste. // The city / has now made local food service businesses / stop using plastic straws, / **spoons**, / forks / and knives. // They can't provide them / to customers / anymore. // Instead, / they have to use / something **eco-friendly**. // Paper straws are good / for this purpose. //

In addition, / paper straws can have many different designs. // They can be printed / with a variety of colors and letters. // Companies can use them / for their advertisements. // I don't think / this is easy / with plastic straws. //

Paper straws are eco-friendly / and really useful. // I hope / more will be used / in other places / in the future. // (188 words)

🔊 **音読しよう**　　　　　　　　　　　　　　　　　スピーキング・トレーナー

Practice 1　スラッシュ位置で文を区切って読んでみよう ☐
Practice 2　音の変化に注意して読んでみよう ☐
TRY!　　　　１分50秒以内に本文全体を音読しよう ☐

📖 **Reading**　本文の内容を読んで理解しよう【知識・技能】【思考力・判断力・表現力】　　　共通テスト

Make the correct choice to complete each sentence or answer each question. (各6点)

1.　The writer of the blog ☐ .

① couldn't drink coffee because it was served without a straw

② didn't like the paper straw because it was not as strong as a plastic one

③ drank an iced coffee with an unusual straw

④ was served an iced coffee with a plastic straw

2.　Which of the following can food shops in Seattle **not** do? ☐

① Keep using eco-friendly goods.

② Serve food with stainless spoons.

③ Provide straws printed their names on.

④ Use plastic forks.

■ 音の変化を理解して音読することができる。　　　　　　　　□ ストローに関する英文を読んで概要や要点を捉えることができる。
■ 文脈を理解して適切な語句を用いて英文を完成することができる。　　○ 平易な英語で話される短い英文を聞いて必要な情報を聞き取ることができる。
■ 環境にやさしい製品について簡単な語句を用いて説明することができる。　○ SNS について簡単な語句を用いて考えを表現することができる。

🔍 Vocabulary & Grammar　重要表現や文法事項について理解しよう【知識】　英検® GTEC®

Make the correct choice to complete each sentence. （各 2 点）

1. This kind of tool is usually made (　　　　) wood and iron.
   ① by　　　　　　② in　　　　　　③ of　　　　　　④ to

2. It's too cold to drink (　　　　) coffee today.
   ① expensive　　　② hot　　　　　③ iced　　　　　④ strong

3. I only have a (　　　　) of water in my bottle.
   ① bit　　　　　　② couple　　　　③ little　　　　④ variety

4. The website will (　　　　) a lot of hints to those who are in trouble.
   ① produce　　　　② project　　　　③ promise　　　④ provide

5. Did he remember when (　　　　) with me at the coffee shop?
   ① did he talk　　 ② he is talking　 ③ he talked　　④ he was talk

🎧 Listening　英文を聞いて理解しよう【知識・技能】【思考力・判断力・表現力】　共通テスト　CD 55

Listen to the English and make the best choice to match the content. （4 点）

① It has been more than three years since the speaker started his blog.

② The speaker has posted his blog for nearly three years.

③ The speaker is going to start his new blog next month.

💬 Interaction　英文を聞いて会話を続けよう【知識・技能】【思考力・判断力・表現力】　スピーキング・トレーナー　CD 56

Listen to the English and respond to the last remark. （7 点）

［メ モ　　　 ］

アドバイス　身の回りのものをよく思い出して，具体例を挙げてみよう。

💬 Production（Speak）　自分の考えを話して伝えよう【思考力・判断力・表現力】　スピーキング・トレーナー

Speak out your answer to the following question. （7 点）

Have you posted messages to a blog or other social media site before? Do you like doing it?

アドバイス　投稿したことがなくても，なぜ投稿しないのかなどの理由を必ず加えよう。

Plastics have made / our lives more convenient, / but plastic waste is / now a global problem / and is getting more and more serious. //

① Our lives largely **depend** on plastics. // They are used / for many everyday goods: / shopping bags, / office **supplies** / and even clothes. // From 1950 to 2015, / about 8.3 billion **tons** of plastics / were created. // About half of that **amount** / was produced / in the last 13 years / of that period, / and people are producing / more and more plastics / every year. //

② What happens / after we throw plastics away? // Some are burned / as garbage, / but most end up / as waste / in **landfills** / or in the natural environment. // In 2015, / the amount of plastic garbage / around the world / reached about 6.3 billion tons. // Such plastic waste can escape / from the land / into the ocean. // The amount is **estimated** / to be more than eight million tons / each year. //

③ However, / that is not the end / of the story. // Plastics in the sea / never disappear. // They continue to **pollute** our water. // Sunlight and waves / break them down / into smaller pieces. // In addition, / dangerous materials / stick to these **microplastics** / in the environment. // These plastic bits **remain** / in the places / where many food **sources** are found. // They can be eaten or **swallowed** / by sea life. // (206 words)

🔊 **音読しよう**　　　　　　　　　　　　　　　　　　スピーキング・トレーナー
　Practice 1　スラッシュ位置で文を区切って読んでみよう ☐
　Practice 2　音の変化に注意して読んでみよう ☐
　TRY!　　　　2分以内に本文全体を音読しよう ☐

📖 **Reading**　本文の内容を読んで理解しよう【知識・技能】【思考力・判断力・表現力】　　　共通テスト

Make the correct choice to complete each sentence or answer each question. (各4点)

1. About 4 million tons of plastics were produced all over the world ☐ .
   ① between 1950 and 2015　　　② between 2000 and 2015
   ③ from 2002 to 2015　　　　　④ until 2015

2. Burned waste plastics are ☐ those going into landfills or the natural environment.
   ① as little as　　② as many as　　③ less than　　④ more than

3. Which of the following are true about plastics in the ocean? (Choose two options. The order does not matter.) ☐ ・ ☐
   ① Fish eat and break them down into pieces.
   ② They are broken down into smaller pieces by sunlight and waves.
   ③ They reached about 6.3 billion tons in 2015.
   ④ They remain in the ocean for a long time polluting the water.

🔍 Vocabulary & Grammar　重要表現や文法事項について理解しよう【知識】　英検◉ GTEC◉

Make the correct choice to complete each sentence. (各2点)

1. The man (　　　　) the hospital after a long period of drinking.
　① ended up in　　　② found out　　　　③ left for　　　　④ resulted to

2. The answer to the question (　　　　) the situation.
　① depends on　　　② gets over　　　　③ runs after　　　④ tends to

3. We need to (　　　　) how much it will cost to start the business.
　① estimate　　　　② pollute　　　　　③ remain　　　　④ supply

4. Don't (　　　　) to your idea.　Look at the matter differently.
　① search　　　　　② spare　　　　　③ stick　　　　④ surprise

5. This is the classroom (　　　　) I take my English class.
　① that　　　　　② where　　　　　③ which　　　　④ who

🎧 Listening　英文を聞いて理解しよう【知識・技能】【思考力・判断力・表現力】　共通テスト　CD 57

Listen to the English and make the best choice to match the content. (4点)

　① People can get plastic bags for free at supermarkets in Paris.

　② The speaker has to pay for single-use plastic bags in Paris.

　③ The speaker didn't know that he couldn't get plastic bags.

🗨 Interaction　英文を聞いて会話を続けよう【知識・技能】【思考力・判断力・表現力】　スピーキング・トレーナー　CD 58

Listen to the English and respond to the last remark. (7点)

［メモ　　　]

　アドバイス　自分の生活を振り返ってみよう。water bottle「水筒」　　plastic bottle「ペットボトル」

✍ Production (Write)　自分の考えを書いて伝えよう【思考力・判断力・表現力】

Write your answer to the following question. (7点)

　Choose one useful plastic product around you and explain it.

　アドバイス　A useful plastic product for me is ... で書き始めるとよい。

----

④ In **Costa Rica**, / a **biologist** tries / to pull out a plastic straw / from a sea turtle's nose. // The turtle is **bleeding**, / and it appears to be / in a lot of pain. // Perhaps it ate the straw / by mistake / and then tried / to throw it up. // Instead of getting out of its mouth, / the straw went into its nose. //

⑤ Sea animals, / including fish and **shellfish**, / can mistake plastics / for food / and swallow them. // The chances are higher / for microplastic pieces. // The animals cannot **digest** plastics / in their stomachs, / and they feel full / all the time. // This makes it difficult / for them / to eat actual food. // As a result, / many animals in the sea / are dying of **starvation**. //

⑥ We humans / can also be influenced / by plastics / in the sea. // Scientists believe / that microplastics are present / in seafood. // Most of them / seem to remain / in the **guts** / of fish and shellfish. // It appears / that they do not move / into the parts / we eat. // However, / the possible **risks** / to food safety and our health / are still not known. // (174 words)

◄)) 音読しよう　　　　　　　　　　　　　　　　　　　スピーキング・トレーナー

Practice 1　スラッシュ位置で文を区切って読んでみよう □
Practice 2　音の変化に注意して読んでみよう □
TRY!　　　　1分40秒以内に本文全体を音読しよう □

📖 Reading　本文の内容を読んで理解しよう【知識・技能】【思考力・判断力・表現力】　　共通テスト

Make the correct choice to complete each sentence. (各4点)

1. It seems that the sea turtle took in a plastic straw ☐.
   ① by a biologist　　　　　　② from its mouth
   ③ from its nose　　　　　　④ on purpose

2. We don't know if microplastics in seafood will ☐ our body.
   ① help　　　　　　　　　　② have a negative effect on
   ③ move into　　　　　　　　④ remain in

3. One **fact** from the paragraphs is that ☐.
   ① plastic pollution in the sea leads to the starvation of sea life
   ② plastics in the sea have something to do with our health
   ③ plastics in the sea have nothing to do with our health
   ④ the turtle felt pain when a biologist was pulling out a plastic straw from its nose

🔍 Vocabulary & Grammar　重要表現や文法事項について理解しよう【知識】　英検® GTEC®

Make the correct choice to complete each sentence.（各2点）

1. The actor died (　　　) cancer at the age of 68.
   ① by　　　　　　　② for　　　　　　③ of　　　　　　④ on

2. I wanted to buy the third book in the series, but I bought the second one (　　　) mistake.
   ① by　　　　　　　② for　　　　　　③ on　　　　　　④ with

3. The elephant looked sleepy, and then (　　　) its house in the zoo.
   ① came across　　② came along　　③ went into　　④ went on

4. I had felt sick until I (　　　) what I ate last night.
   ① brought about　② caught up　　③ gave back　　④ threw up

5. I found (　　　) to stock up on food and drink for the typhoon.
   ① importance　　② important　　③ it importance　④ it important

🎧 Listening　英文を聞いて理解しよう【知識・技能】【思考力・判断力・表現力】　共通テスト　CD 59

Listen to the English and make the best choice to match the content.（4点）

① Seafood is the speaker's favorite food.

② The speaker didn't like seafood before.

③ The speaker doesn't want to have seafood anymore.

💬 Interaction　英文を聞いて会話を続けよう【知識・技能】【思考力・判断力・表現力】　スピーキング・トレーナー　CD 60

Listen to the English and respond to the last remark.（7点）

［メモ　　　]

アドバイス　最初の発言は自分の発言なので，見たことがない場合でも海洋汚染について何か知っていることを言おう。

✎ Production（Write）　自分の考えを書いて伝えよう【思考力・判断力・表現力】

Write your answer to the following question.（7点）

Give your idea to decrease the number of animals dying from eating plastic garbage.

アドバイス　実現できるかどうかを考慮する必要はないので，思いついたアイデアを書こう。

----

⑦ What can we do / to stop plastic pollution? // One solution is / to use "**biodegradable**" plastics. // They can break down / into water and **carbon dioxide** (CO_2) / and finally **blend** with the environment. // However, / they may not work / in that way / in dark, cool and low-**oxygen** places, / such as in the sea. // For that reason, / biodegradable plastics / may not be the best solution, / although they can be part of it. //

⑧ Another solution is recycling. // Some countries are successful / in **promoting** it. // In Norway, / for example, / people can return plastic bottles / to supermarkets / and get a **refund** / for them. // This system / has pushed the country's plastic bottle recycling rate / to over 95 percent. // Across the world, / however, / only 9 percent of used plastics / are recycled. //

⑨ What seems important, then, / is cutting the amount / of plastics / we use. // To achieve this, / many businesses / around the world / are no longer using **single-use** plastics. // Plastic-waste control is / not only about / how we should make and recycle plastics. // It is also about / how we should use plastics. // (170 words)

🔊 **音読しよう**

スピーキング・トレーナー

Practice 1 スラッシュ位置で文を区切って読んでみよう ☐
Practice 2 音の変化に注意して読んでみよう ☐
TRY!   1分40秒以内に本文全体を音読しよう ☐

📖 **Reading** 本文の内容を読んで理解しよう【知識・技能】【思考力・判断力・表現力】 共通テスト

Make the correct choice to complete each sentence or answer each question. (各4点)

1. A weak point of biodegradable plastics is that ☐ .

   ① it will cost a lot to make them

   ② they aren't useful at all to solve pollution

   ③ they can't work well in the sea   ④ they might give off too much CO_2

2. Which of the following is **not** true about Norway's efforts? ☐

   ① In Norway, nine percent of plastic bottles are recycled.

   ② More than nineteen out of twenty plastic bottles are collected for recycling.

   ③ Norway is successful in its effort to recycle plastic bottles.

   ④ The recycling rate in Norway is far higher than average.

3. To stop plastic pollution, ☐ .

   ① all we have to think about is recycling plastic products

   ② biodegradable plastics will be the best solution

   ③ efforts should be made by consumers, not by companies

   ④ reduction of the amount of plastics we use seems to be important

🔍 Vocabulary & Grammar　重要表現や文法事項について理解しよう【知識】　英検◎ GTEC◎

Make the correct choice to complete each sentence. (各2点)

1. The sound of the bell was hard to hear when it (　　　) the surrounding noise.
   ① blended with　② came together　③ combined to　④ mixed

2. The scientists are sure to be successful (　　　) creating new cancer medicine.
   ① in　② of　③ on　④ to

3. The romance movie is no (　　　) presented at theaters in this area.
   ① later　② larger　③ less　④ longer

4. The long cold summer (　　　) the price of vegetables to the highest ever.
   ① left　② made　③ pushed　④ rose

5. I (　　　) for her to lose her way in Tokyo.
   ① think I'm natural　② think it natural
   ③ thinking it natural　④ thought natural

🎧 Listening　英文を聞いて理解しよう【知識・技能】【思考力・判断力・表現力】　共通テスト　CD 61

Listen to the English and make the best choice to match the content. (4点)

① About thirty of the collected bottles were thrown away in the speaker's country.
② The speaker collected some plastic bottles on beaches in foreign countries.
③ The speaker found about sixty foreign plastic bottles on the beach.

💬 Interaction　英文を聞いて会話を続けよう【知識・技能】【思考力・判断力・表現力】　スピーキング・トレーナー　CD 62

Listen to the English and respond to the last remark. (7点)

[メモ　　　　　　　　　　　　　　　　　　　　　　]

アドバイス　何についてたずねられているかを注意して聞き取ろう。

✏️ Production (Write)　自分の考えを書いて伝えよう【思考力・判断力・表現力】

Write your answer to the following question. (7点)

Do you agree that supermarkets sell meat or fish in single-use plastic containers? Why or why not?

アドバイス　賛成か反対かをサポートする自分の考えをしっかりまとめよう。

You are doing some research / on the plastic-waste problem. // On the Internet, / you have found an article / about a **discovery** / made by a group of scientists. //

Can Plastic-Eating **Bacteria** Save the Earth? //

Back in 2016, / "PET-eating" bacteria were found. // PET is a plastic / widely used / in drink bottles. // Now a group of scientists / has developed a new **enzyme** / from the bacteria. // It can break PET down / more quickly. // While PET takes hundreds of years / to break down / in nature, / the enzyme, / called PETase, / can start the **process** / in just a few days. //

The discovery came / by chance / when the scientists were looking / into the enzyme. // They found / that the performance of PETase / could be improved / by changing its **surface structure**. // The improved enzyme / was also tested / on another plastic, PEF. // This plastic is also slow / to break down / in nature. // The result was surprising. // The enzyme worked better / on PEF / than on PET. // The scientists are now trying / to make the enzyme work / even better. // They hope / that future varieties can work / on other kinds / of plastics. //

PETase could be a solution / to the problem / of recycling plastics. // Plastic materials lose some quality / each time they are recycled. // Bottles become clothes, / then carpets, / and finally, waste. // The recycling circle is not closed. // However, / PETase may be able to close the circle. // It can turn plastics / back into their original materials. // Thanks to this, / plastics may be used / again and again / without losing quality. // Although this technology hasn't reached **practical** use yet, / it may give us a hint / about how to solve the plastic-waste problem. // (264 words)

🔊 **音読しよう**　　　　　　　　　　　　　　　　　　　　　スピーキング・トレーナー
Practice 1　スラッシュ位置で文を区切って読んでみよう ☐
Practice 2　音の変化に注意して読んでみよう ☐
TRY!　　　　2分40秒以内に本文全体を音読しよう ☐

📖 **Reading**　本文の内容を読んで理解しよう【知識・技能】【思考力・判断力・表現力】　共通テスト

Make the correct choice to complete each sentence. (各6点)

1. The enzyme called PETase ☐ .

   ① can break PET down twice as quickly as before

   ② finishes breaking PET down in a few days

   ③ was discovered by scientists in 2016　④ was originally found in nature

2. At this time, PETase **cannot** ☐ .

   ① be improved by research and new technologies

   ② improve the quality of plastic materials

   ③ return plastics into their original materials

   ④ work on materials other than PET

🔊 音の変化を理解して音読することができる。
📖 科学者のある発見に関する英文を読んで概要や要点を捉えることができる。
🔍 文脈を理解して適切な語句を用いて英文を完成することができる。　🎧 やや長めの英文を聞いて必要な情報を聞き取ることができる。

als

🔍 Vocabulary & Grammar　重要表現や文法事項について理解しよう【知識】　英検 ® GTEC ®

Make the correct choice to complete each sentence. (各 2 点)

1. When you get into trouble, stop and look (　　　) its cause.
   ① after　　　　　② down　　　　　③ into　　　　　④ out

2. It is very easy to (　　　) the ice back into the water.
   ① do　　　　　② get　　　　　③ take　　　　　④ turn

3. (　　　) you start to use the Internet, you need to type in your account and password.
   ① All time　　　② Each time　　　③ Short time　　　④ Some time

4. (　　　) of years have passed since the death of the great musician.
   ① A hundred　　② Hundred　　③ Hundreds　　④ The hundreds

5. I found the old map (　　　) chance at a secondhand bookstore in Kanda.
   ① by　　　　　② from　　　　　③ in　　　　　④ with

6. I make it a rule (　　　) English novels while I go to school.
   ① read　　　　② reading　　　③ to be read　　　④ to read

7. The time will come (　　　) you'll understand what I told you.
   ① how　　　　② that　　　　③ when　　　　④ why

8. Let me show you the reason (　　　) the accident took place.
   ① how　　　　② of　　　　③ of why　　　　④ why

🎧 Listening　英文を聞いて理解しよう【知識・技能】【思考力・判断力・表現力】　共通テスト　CD 63

Listen to the English and make the best choice to match the content. (各 4 点)

1. In the London Marathon in 2019, runners received drinking water 　　　 .
   ① in paper cups　　　　　　② in plastic bags
   ③ in plastic bottles　　　　　④ without plastic bottles

2. Which of the following is true about the London Marathon in 2019?
   ① The runners could eat the plastic bottle if they liked.
   ② The runners didn't receive drinking water.
   ③ The runners joined the race to try Ooho.
   ④ The runners never threw a bottle away while running.

3. Which of the following is true about Ooho?
   ① Its developer had student members in the beginning.
   ② It was invented in 2019 by a company in London.
   ③ It is used to pack plants from the sea.
   ④ It will be used for packaging alcoholic drinks soon.

You are walking / on a street. // You find a poster / of an interesting event. //

The International Center in Tokyo / will host a special talk. //

Living with Hiroshima: My Memories //

　Koko Kondo was born / in Hiroshima / in 1944. // She experienced the atomic bombing / when she was just eight months old. // After she grew up, / Koko became a **storyteller**. // She has shared her own experiences / with a lot of people, / from small children / to older people. // She gives her talks / both in Japanese / and in English. // She has received many prizes / for her excellent work / as a peace **advocate**. //

1:30 p.m. on Saturday, July 2, 2022 //

◆ Building K, Room 303 //

◆ **Admission** Free //

◆ Information: 0123-45-xxxx //

　　　　　　https://www.ictokyo.ac.jp/peace //

About the Talk //

　After World War II, / Koko remained angry / with those who **destroyed** Hiroshima. // However, / a chance to see an American man / changed her life. // He was the **co-pilot** / of the plane / that dropped the atomic bomb / on Hiroshima. // When she saw his deep **regret**, / Koko realized / what she really hated / was not the person / in front of her / but war itself. // Her story gives us a chance / to reflect on our thoughts / about war. //　(192 words)

🔊 **音読しよう**
　Practice 1　スラッシュ位置で文を区切って読んでみよう ☐
　Practice 2　音の変化に注意して読んでみよう ☐
　TRY!　　　 ２分以内に本文全体を音読しよう ☐

スピーキング・トレーナー

📖 **Reading**　本文の内容を読んで理解しよう【知識・技能】【思考力・判断力・表現力】　共通テスト

Make the correct choice to complete each sentence or answer each question. (各6点)

1.　Koko Kondo is a storyteller 　　　　.

　① who has shared her story in English

　② who received few prizes for her work

　③ who was born eight months after the atomic bombing

　④ whose audience has always been younger than her

🔊 音の変化を理解して音読することができる。　　　📖 講演会に関する英文を読んで概要や要点を捉えることができる。
🔍 文脈を理解して適切な語句を用いて英文を完成することができる。　　🎧 平易な英語で話される短い英文を聞いて必要な情報を聞き取ることができる。
🎙 スピーチを聞いた経験について簡単な語句を用いて説明することができる。　💬 怒りについて簡単な語句を用いて考えを表現することができる。

oals

2. Which information is **not** known from the poster? ☐

① E-mail address of the event site.

② The price the audience will have to pay for the event.

③ The room number of the event site.

④ What Koko Kondo will talk about.

🔍 Vocabulary & Grammar　重要表現や文法事項について理解しよう【知識】　　英検® GTEC®

Make the correct choice to complete each sentence. (各2点)

1. When you decide on your future job, you'd better ( ) on what you have studied.

① effect　　　　② protest　　　　③ reflect　　　　④ respect

2. I'm very ( ) with him for what he said to me.

① absent　　　　② afraid　　　　③ angry　　　　④ attractive

3. I should have taken that route. I deeply ( ) my decision.

① collect　　　　② estimate　　　　③ reflect　　　　④ regret

4. Because of the typhoon, a large area of the village was ( ).

① destroyed　　　　② elected　　　　③ extinct　　　　④ patient

5. It ( ) to rain when I went to bed last night.

① had began　　　　② had begun　　　　③ has began　　　　④ have begun

🎧 Listening　英文を聞いて理解しよう【知識・技能】【思考力・判断力・表現力】　　共通テスト CD 64

Listen to the English and make the best choice to match the content. (4点)

① The speaker heard about the event from someone else.

② The speaker shared the information about the event with other people.

③ The speaker will know about the event soon.

💬 Interaction　英文を聞いて会話を続けよう【知識・技能】【思考力・判断力・表現力】　スピーキング・トレーナー CD 65

Listen to the English and respond to the last remark. (7点)

[メモ 　　　　　　　　　　　　　　　　　　　　　　　　　　　　　　　]

アドバイス　講演会だけでなく，動画サイトで聞いたことがあるものなども含めて思い出してみよう。

💬 Production (Speak)　自分の考えを話して伝えよう【思考力・判断力・表現力】　スピーキング・トレーナー

Speak out your answer to the following question. (7点)

When you are angry with someone or something, what do you do to calm down?

アドバイス　自分が怒っているときにどうしているか思い出してみよう。

Why do the *hibakusha* talk / about the war? // What can we learn / from them? // What stories need to be passed on / to the next generations? //

① Two atomic bombs were dropped / on Japan / in August 1945. // About 140,000 people / in Hiroshima / and about 70,000 people / in Nagasaki / had died / by the end of the year. // Seventy-one years later, / in May 2016, / Barack Obama became the first sitting president / to visit Hiroshima. // He made a speech there / and told the world / the importance / of giving up **nuclear weapons**. //

② In his speech, / President Obama **referred** to a woman / who had **forgiven** a pilot / who dropped the atomic bomb / on Hiroshima. // The woman's name / is Koko Kondo. // She has shared her story / as a *hibakusha*, / a **surviving victim** / of the atomic bombings. // Obama's speech / helped her activities / gain **worldwide recognition**. //

③ Koko's father, / Kiyoshi Tanimoto, / was a famous **pastor** / who also survived the bombing. // He is one of the main characters / in *Hiroshima*, / a book / written by John Hersey. // The war left many young women / injured by the atomic bomb. // Kiyoshi helped them / receive **medical** care / in the United States. // He had a great influence / on Koko. // If he were alive now, / what would he say / to his daughter? /

(207 words)

🔊 音読しよう

Practice 1 スラッシュ位置で文を区切って読んでみよう ☐

Practice 2 音の変化に注意して読んでみよう ☐

TRY! 2分以内に本文全体を音読しよう ☐

スピーキング・トレーナー

📖 **Reading** 本文の内容を読んで理解しよう【知識・技能】【思考力・判断力・表現力】 共通テスト

Make the correct choice to complete each sentence or answer each question. (各4点)

1. Victims of the atomic bombing in Nagasaki in 1945 were ☐ those in Hiroshima.

   ① about as many as ② about half as many as

   ③ about twice as many as ④ much more than

2. In his speech, Barack Obama stressed most ☐.

   ① that nuclear weapons were unnecessary

   ② the importance of nuclear weapons

   ③ the personality of Koko Kondo ④ why the U.S. held nuclear weapons

3. Which of the following is true about Koko Kondo? ☐

   ① Her activities became more known thanks to Obama.

   ② John Hersey featured her in his book called *Hiroshima*.

   ③ Thanks to her efforts, young women could receive medical care in the U.S.

   ④ The atomic bombing in Hiroshima killed her father.

🔍 Vocabulary & Grammar　重要表現や文法事項について理解しよう【知識】　英検◎ GTEC◎

Make the correct choice to complete each sentence. (各2点)

1. The reporter (　　　) to the floods in the past to draw people's attention.
   ① occurred　　　② offered　　　③ preferred　　　④ referred

2. The pandemic of the disease made him (　　　) up the idea of studying abroad.
   ① give　　　② make　　　③ save　　　④ turn

3. People's early experiences usually have a great (　　　) on their later lives.
   ① difference　　　② influence　　　③ preference　　　④ sentence

4. In this club, the older members have (　　　) maintenance of its official website to the younger members.
   ① gotten over　　　② looked upon　　　③ passed on　　　④ turned down

5. I would never do such a thing if I (　　　) in your position.
   ① am　　　② be　　　③ did　　　④ were

🎧 Listening　英文を聞いて理解しよう【知識・技能】【思考力・判断力・表現力】　共通テスト CD 66

Listen to the English and make the best choice to match the content. (4点)

① The speaker has seen the U.S. president on a TV program.

② The speaker has been seen to make a presentation.

③ The U.S. president watched the speaker on TV.

💬 Interaction　英文を聞いて会話を続けよう【知識・技能】【思考力・判断力・表現力】　スピーキング・トレーナー CD 67

Listen to the English and respond to the last remark. (7点)

［メモ　　　　　　　　　　　　　　　　　　　　　　　　　　　　　　　　　　　]

アドバイス　質問の there が何を指すのかに注意して，Yes の場合はいつ行ったか，No の場合は行きたいかどうかなどを答えよう。

✏ Production (Write)　自分の考えを書いて伝えよう【思考力・判断力・表現力】

Write your answer to the following question. (7点)

When did you first learn about the atomic bombings in Hiroshima and Nagasaki? And how did you feel then?

アドバイス　「いつ知ったか」と「どのように感じたか」の2点が聞かれている。I felt sad to know that ... 「…と知って悲しく感じた」などの表現を使ってみよう。

4　**Fortunately**, / Koko's family survived the bombing, / although they had to face / the terrible realities / of the war. // They saw many people / come to their church: / women with terrible burns / on their faces, / children who had lost their families, / and people suffering from the **aftereffects** / of the bomb. // At that time, / Koko couldn't help thinking, / "If the Americans had not dropped / the atomic bomb, / we wouldn't have gone through this terribly painful experience." //

5　Koko had long wanted / to **avenge** the victims, / and a chance actually came / when she was ten years old. // She got the chance / to visit America / and appear on a TV show / featuring her father. // The program / **secretly** planned a meeting / between her family and Captain Robert Lewis, / the co-pilot / of the Enola Gay. //

6　At first, / Koko thought / she would kick and **bite** Lewis, / but the next moment, / she was surprised / to see the pilot's eyes / filled with tears. // He remembered the bombing / and said, / "My God, / what have we done?" // He **bitterly** regretted / carrying out the bombing order. // In that moment, / Koko realized / the pilot was also a victim / of war. // (184 words)

🔊 音読しよう　　　　　　　　　　　　　　　　　　　スピーキング・トレーナー
Practice 1　スラッシュ位置で文を区切って読んでみよう □
Practice 2　音の変化に注意して読んでみよう □
TRY!　　　　１分50秒以内に本文全体を音読しよう □

📖 **Reading**　本文の内容を読んで理解しよう【知識・技能】【思考力・判断力・表現力】　　共通テスト

Make the correct choice to complete each sentence or answer each question. (各4点)

1. It was ☐ before the start of the program that Koko's family would meet Robert Lewis.

　① featured　　　② hidden　　　③ shown　　　④ surprised

2. Lewis' eyes were full of tears when he remembered ☐ .

　① seeing Koko's family

　② that he had been kicked by Koko

　③ the moment the war ended

　④ what he had done before

3. Which of the following is true about Koko's experience? ☐

　① She avenged the victims.

　② She got a chance to meet Robert Lewis.

　③ She kicked the pilot of the Enola Gay.

　④ She regretted seeing Robert Lewis.

🔍 Vocabulary & Grammar　重要表現や文法事項について理解しよう【知識】　　英検◎ GTEC◎

Make the correct choice to complete each sentence.（各2点）

1.　The man has (　　　) from back pain since he had a traffic accident.

　① caught　　　　② gotten　　　　③ suffered　　　　④ troubled

2.　The long letter from her mother was (　　　) with love.

　① covered　　　　② filled　　　　③ great　　　　④ satisfied

3.　After I saw the movie, I couldn't (　　　) reading the original work.

　① go　　　　② help　　　　③ miss　　　　④ try

4.　(　　　), there were no victims and no injured people.

　① Following　　　　② Formally　　　　③ Fortunately　　　　④ Further

5.　If she (　　　) more money, she could have paid for the travel to Europe.

　① had saved　　　② had been saved　　③ has saved　　④ would have saved

🎧 Listening　英文を聞いて理解しよう【知識・技能】【思考力・判断力・表現力】　　共通テスト CD 68

Listen to the English and make the best choice to match the content.（4点）

　① Susan was asked to meet Tom on a TV program.

　② Tom and Susan didn't want to appear on TV.

　③ Tom ended up meeting Susan on a TV program.

💬 Interaction　英文を聞いて会話を続けよう【知識・技能】【思考力・判断力・表現力】　スピーキング・トレーナー CD 69

Listen to the English and respond to the last remark.（7点）

［メモ　　　　　　　　　　　　　　　　　　　　　　　　　　　　　　　　　　　　］

　アドバイス　相手の発話を参考にしながら，自分の経験を述べよう。

✍ Production（Write）　自分の考えを書いて伝えよう【思考力・判断力・表現力】

Write your answer to the following question.（7点）

　If your close friend lost something important, such as a pet, what would you do for him/her?

　アドバイス　相手の気持ちに寄り添えるような行動を考えよう。「〜してあげるだろう」はI would 〜を使おう。

7 That important event / changed Koko's way / of thinking. // She wrote / in her book later, / "If I had not met Captain Robert Lewis, / I might have become a person / who never forgives others." // She then began to realize / the **necessity** / of spreading the memory / of the war / from person to person. // This was the beginning / of her **lifework** / as a storyteller / and peace advocate. //

8 The stories told by the *hibakusha*, / including Koko's, / have been received / in many ways / by younger people. // Some of them / have also become new storytellers / who hand down the stories / of the *hibakusha*. // Others try to express / the **horrors** of war / by painting, / acting / or giving music performances. // They all believe / that the experiences of the *hibakusha* / need to be shared / with future generations. //

9 Someday, / we will no longer be able to hear / the living voices / of the *hibakusha*. // However, / the memories of August 6 and 9, 1945, / must never **fade** away. // As Japan is the only country / that has ever suffered / atomic bomb attacks, / each of us has a **responsibility** / to hand down the memories / of the war / to future generations. // In the future, / how will you share / what you know / about war? // (197 words)

🔊 **音読しよう**　　　　　　　　　　　　　　　　　　　スピーキング・トレーナー
Practice 1　スラッシュ位置で文を区切って読んでみよう ☐
Practice 2　音の変化に注意して読んでみよう ☐
TRY!　　　2分以内に本文全体を音読しよう ☐

📖 **Reading**　本文の内容を読んで理解しよう【知識・技能】【思考力・判断力・表現力】　　共通テスト

Make the correct choice to complete each sentence or answer each question. (各4点)

1. Which of the following are true about Koko? (Choose two options. The order does not matter.) ☐ · ☐

   ① She became a storyteller right after she met with Captain Lewis.

   ② She gave up writing about her experiences.

   ③ She is a person who can forgive other people.

   ④ The meeting with Captain Lewis changed her mind.

2. ☐ is **not** taken as an example of artists influenced by the stories of the *hibakusha*.

   ① The actor　　② The movie director　　③ The musician　　④ The painter

3. The time will come when we ☐ .

   ① experience an atomic bombing again

   ② forget the memories of August 6 and 9 in 1945

   ③ lose a chance to meet the *hibakusha*

   ④ see all the countries that have atomic bombs give them up

🔍 Vocabulary & Grammar　重要表現や文法事項について理解しよう【知識】　英検® GTEC®

Make the correct choice to complete each sentence. (各2点)

1. Water is an absolute (　　　) in our lives.
   ① necessarily　　② necessary　　③ necessity　　④ needed

2. There was an expression of (　　　) on his face.
   ① afraid　　② horror　　③ scary　　④ terrible

3. The paint on the wall has (　　　) after a long time.
   ① faded away　　② passed away　　③ run away　　④ thrown away

4. We should maintain and (　　　) down the old castle for future generations.
   ① go　　② hand　　③ put　　④ turn

5. The manager of the factory let the group (　　　) the factory.
   ① enter　　② entered　　③ entering　　④ to enter

🎧 Listening　英文を聞いて理解しよう【知識・技能】【思考力・判断力・表現力】　共通テスト　CD 70

Listen to the English and make the best choice to match the content. (4点)

① One of the twenty books was written by the speaker.

② There are twenty stories on world peace written by the speaker.

③ The speaker's story is one of the twenty.

💬 Interaction　英文を聞いて会話を続けよう【知識・技能】【思考力・判断力・表現力】　スピーキング・トレーナー　CD 71

Listen to the English and respond to the last remark. (7点)

［メモ　　　　　　　　　　　　　　　　　　　　　　　　　　　　　　　　　　］

アドバイス　知っているものがなくても，会話を続けるための言葉を加えよう。

✐ Production (Write)　自分の考えを書いて伝えよう【思考力・判断力・表現力】

Write your answer to the following question. (7点)

Why is it necessary to share the experience of war with younger generations? Write your ideas.

アドバイス　「なぜ必要か」を考えるときは，それがなかった場合どうなるかを想像すると書きやすい。tragic experience「悲惨な経験」。

You are listening to a **discussion** / about the **definition** / of peace. //

Teacher: The definition of peace / can **differ** / among us. // A dictionary may **define** it / as a state or period / without war. // If so, / the **opposite** word / of peace / will be war. // However, / not all of us / agree with this definition / as we may not feel **peaceful** / even when we are not fighting / each other. // How would you define peace? // Discuss it / in your group. //

Mika: I define peace / as a state / of having the necessities / for life. // If we didn't have enough food, / **clothing** / and housing, / it would be difficult / to live. // Having the necessities / for life / is the basis / of peace, / I believe. //

Satoshi: I agree with Mika, / but I also think of peace / as a state / of being safe. // Nobody wants to have car accidents. // Nobody wants to be attacked / when they are walking / at night. // Safety must be part of peace. // What do you think, Emily? //

Emily: **Um**, personally, / I feel peaceful / when I'm having a meal / with my family / or talking / with my friends. // That is not something special / at all. // Just being able to spend a normal life / means peace / to me. //

Satoshi: I like your idea, Emily. // Although we don't usually notice that, / we may have peace already / in our life. // (213 words)

🔊 **音読しよう**　　　　　　　　　　　　　　　スピーキング・トレーナー

Practice 1　スラッシュ位置で文を区切って読んでみよう ☐
Practice 2　音の変化に注意して読んでみよう ☐
TRY!　　　2分10秒以内に本文全体を音読しよう ☐

📖 **Reading**　本文の内容を読んで理解しよう【知識・技能】【思考力・判断力・表現力】　　共通テスト

Make the correct choice to complete each sentence. (各6点)

1. ☐ thinks highly of the state of not being dangerous.
   ① Emily　　　　　　　　② Mika
   ③ Satoshi　　　　　　　④ Teacher

2. ☐ and ☐ refer to food in their remarks about peace. (The order does not matter.)
   ① Emily　　　　　　　　② Mika
   ③ Satoshi　　　　　　　④ Teacher

🔊 音の変化を理解して音読することができる。
📖 平和の定義に関する英文を読んで概要や要点を捉えることができる。
🔍 文脈を理解して適切な語句を用いて英文を完成することができる。　　🎧 やや長めの英文を聞いて必要な情報を聞き取ることができる。

als

🔍 Vocabulary & Grammar　重要表現や文法事項について理解しよう【知識】　　英検® GTEC®

Make the correct choice to complete each sentence. (各2点)

1. The (　　　) side of the Earth from Japan isn't Brazil, but the sea off Brazil.
   ① object　　　　　② opposite　　　　　③ out　　　　　④ overseas

2. If a war broke out in Asia, our (　　　) lives would be lost.
   ① diary　　　　　② peaceful　　　　　③ piece of　　　　　④ usually

3. We cannot (　　　) with the development plan.　It won't be good for the environment.
   ① accept　　　　　② agree　　　　　③ satisfy　　　　　④ thank

4. We are going to have a (　　　) with international students about nuclear weapons.
   ① battle　　　　　② discussion　　　　　③ fight　　　　　④ talking

5. The boxing rule (　　　) a heavyweight as a boxer of more than 200 pounds.
   ① decides　　　　　② defines　　　　　③ says　　　　　④ sets

6. If I (　　　) a camera with me at the party, I could have taken some pictures.
   ① had　　　　　② had had　　　　　③ have　　　　　④ have had

7. We could walk to school if it (　　　) now.
   ① hadn't rained　　② isn't raining　　③ rained　　④ weren't raining

8. If I could sing better, I could (　　　) a professional singer.
   ① be able to be　　② become　　③ have become　　④ have being

🎧 Listening　英文を聞いて理解しよう【知識・技能】【思考力・判断力・表現力】　　共通テスト 🎧CD 72

Listen to the English and make the best choice to match the content. (各4点)

1. What happened in 1918?
   ① Mandela began to take Christian education.
   ② Mandela graduated from university.
   ③ Mandela took part in the ANC activities.　④ Mandela was born in South Africa.

2. Why were leaders of the ANC arrested by the South African government?
   ① Because the ANC made the apartheid system.
   ② Because Nelson Mandela was a doctor of law.
   ③ Because their thoughts were violent.
   ④ Because they told Nelson Mandela to join the ANC.

3. When was Nelson Mandela released from prison?
   ① Four months before he won the Nobel Peace Prize.
   ② In 1993.
   ③ Twenty-seven years after his graduation.
   ④ When he was 71.

One morning, / you read an advertisement / about a new supermarket. // You go there / and then listen to an announcement / at the supermarket. //

Welcome to *Amazing Supermarket!* // Now Open in Your Town! //
A unique new supermarket opens / in your town today! //
· No need to bring money. // · No waiting in line / to pay for your shopping. //
Come and enjoy shopping / at our first store / in your town! //
Here is how you shop / at our supermarket: //

1. **Install** the *Amazing Supermarket* application / in your smartphone / before you come. //
2. Bring your smartphone with you / instead of money. //
3. Enter *Amazing Supermarket*. // Touch your smartphone / on the reader / at the entrance. //
4. Start your shopping. // Put the items you want / into your shopping bag. // You can return them / to their original places / if you change your mind. //
5. Go back to the entrance / where you came in, / and just walk out / with the items. //
6. Check your smartphone / after shopping. // Your **receipt** will arrive soon / after you leave *Amazing Supermarket*. //

For more information, / please contact us: / https://www.amazingsupermarket.com //
Tel.: (888)-550-xxxx // Visit our first shop / at 8th Street, / Washington St. 22885. //

Good morning, customers. // Thank you very much / for visiting *Amazing Supermarket* / on opening day. // Before you start shopping, / just a couple of things / to remember. //

When you touch your smartphone / on the phone reader, / please make sure / that your *Amazing Supermarket* application / has been started successfully. // After you choose an item, / if you decide to return it, / please put it back / in its original place. //

We're having an opening sale / for one week. // All items are 20% off / from our usual price, / so don't miss this chance! // Enjoy your shopping! // (279 words)

🔊 **音読しよう**　　　　　　　　　　　　　　　　　　　スピーキング・トレーナー

Practice 1　スラッシュ位置で文を区切って読んでみよう☐
Practice 2　音の変化に注意して読んでみよう☐
TRY!　　　　2分50秒以内に本文全体を音読しよう☐

📖 **Reading**　本文の内容を読んで理解しよう【知識・技能】【思考力・判断力・表現力】　　共通テスト

Make the correct choice to complete each sentence. (各6点)

1. The shopping items will probably be paid for 　　　.
   ① at the same time that you enter the supermarket
   ② every time you put an item in the shopping bag
   ③ when you leave the store
   ④ when you touch the smartphone screen

2. When you don't want to buy what you once put in your shopping bag, you ☐.

① can return it by putting it in the box at the exit

② have to ask for cancellation from the store staff

③ just put it back in its original shelf or case ④ need to go back to the entrance

🔍 Vocabulary & Grammar   重要表現や文法事項について理解しよう【知識】   英検® GTEC®

Make the correct choice to complete each sentence. (各2点)

1. It's Saturday today. (   ) sure that the train will leave at the same time as usual before you go out.

   ① Be   ② Do   ③ Have   ④ Make

2. Don't forget to receive the (   ) at the dental clinic.

   ① receipt   ② reception   ③ recipe   ④ recipient

3. There are a (   ) of birds on the tree over there.

   ① couple   ② hundreds   ③ part   ④ some

4. Let me pay (   ) dinner tonight. You helped me a lot today.

   ① at   ② for   ③ on   ④ with

5. I feel it (   ) for you to prepare for the heavy snow.

   ① hardly   ② importance   ③ necessary   ④ need

🎧 Listening   英文を聞いて理解しよう【知識・技能】【思考力・判断力・表現力】   共通テスト   CD 73

Listen to the English and make the best choice to match the content. (4点)

   ① An email newsletter is one of the options the store offers.

   ② Customers prefer to send email newsletters online.

   ③ The store uses the Internet to take orders from customers.

💬 Interaction   英文を聞いて会話を続けよう【知識・技能】【思考力・判断力・表現力】 スピーキング・トレーナー   CD 74

Listen to the English and respond to the last remark. (7点)

   [メモ   ]

   アドバイス   自分たちがどこに行こうとしているかを踏まえて自分の意見を述べよう。

💬 Production (Speak)   自分の考えを話して伝えよう【思考力・判断力・表現力】   スピーキング・トレーナー

Speak out your answer to the following question. (7点)

   Do you like cashless payments? Why or why not?

   アドバイス   cashless payment は「キャッシュレス決済」のこと。

AI, / or **artificial intelligence**, / is one of the hottest topics / in our society today. // Have you ever used AI technology? // Have you ever been to places / where AI technology is used? //

① You see a colorful advertisement / in your morning newspaper. // While you are looking it over, / your eyes stop / on this sentence: / "No waiting in line / to pay for your shopping." // Getting interested in this new store, / you decide / to buy some things there. //

② Before you go to *Amazing Supermarket*, / you need to **download** an application / **onto** your smartphone. // This is necessary / in order to create your **account** / and **allow cashless** shopping / in the store. // When you arrive / at the supermarket, / you need to touch your smartphone / on the phone reader / at the entrance. // Then your shopping record becomes active / and you are ready / to do your shopping. //

③ Although you may not notice, / while you are shopping, / many small cameras and **sensors** / which have different purposes / are tracking you / all over the store. // These devices sense the items / you pick up / and automatically add them / to your smartphone shopping list. // **Meanwhile**, / any item you return / to its shelf / is **removed** / from the list. // You think, / "I understand! // This is AI!" // You have just remembered the news / you heard / a few days ago. // "AI is operating this store," / the news said. // (220 words)

🔊 **音読しよう**

Practice 1　スラッシュ位置で文を区切って読んでみよう ☐

Practice 2　音の変化に注意して読んでみよう ☐

TRY!　　　 2分10秒以内に本文全体を音読しよう ☐

スピーキング・トレーナー

📖 **Reading**　本文の内容を読んで理解しよう【知識・技能】【思考力・判断力・表現力】　　共通テスト

Make the correct choice to complete each sentence or answer each question. (各 4 点)

1. According to the advertisement mentioned in paragraph 1, you can pay ☐ waiting.

　① along with　　　　　　　② by

　③ out of　　　　　　　　 ④ without

2. To get ready to shop at *Amazing Supermarket*, you have to ☐ first.

　① let your phone shop cashless　　② prepare an app

　③ record your shopping　　　　　 ④ set up an account

3. Which of the following is true? ☐

    ① Cameras in the store see what is added to the shopping list.

    ② If you remove an item from the shopping list, it will return to the shelf automatically.

    ③ Small cameras and sensors in the store sense what you are going to buy.

    ④ You can find out what the sensors in the store are doing.

🔍 Vocabulary & Grammar　重要表現や文法事項について理解しよう【知識】　　英検® GTEC®

Make the correct choice to complete each sentence. (各2点)

1. She (　　　) up some oranges from the basket and handed them to me.

    ① kicked　　　　② picked　　　　③ pulled　　　　④ raised

2. Mr. White (　　　) Mary's report and told her to write it again.

    ① looked　　　　② looked after　　　③ looked for　　　④ looked over

3. I try not to use food containing (　　　) sweeteners when I cook.

    ① art　　　　　② article　　　　③ artificial　　　　④ artist

4. A lot of high schools don't (　　　) students to have a part-time job.

    ① agree　　　　② allow　　　　③ forgive　　　　④ let

5. (　　　) at the station, they went to the ticket counter.

    ① Arrive　　　　② Arrived　　　　③ Arriving　　　　④ Have arrived

🎧 Listening　英文を聞いて理解しよう【知識・技能】【思考力・判断力・表現力】　共通テスト CD 75

Listen to the English and make the best choice to match the content. (4点)

    ① Half of the applications in the speaker's smartphone were installed just now.

    ② The speaker probably removed unnecessary apps from his smartphone.

    ③ The speaker's smartphone has no applications in it.

💬 Interaction　英文を聞いて会話を続けよう【知識・技能】【思考力・判断力・表現力】　スピーキング・トレーナー CD 76

Listen to the English and respond to the last remark. (7点)

[メモ　　　　　　　　　　　　　　　　　　　　　　　　　　　　　　　　　　　]

アドバイス　AI を使った製品が会話のトピックである。

✍ Production（Write）　自分の考えを書いて伝えよう【思考力・判断力・表現力】

Write your answer to the following question. (7点)

    Do you like the shopping system of *Amazing Supermarket*? Why or why not?

    アドバイス　読んだことをもとに，自分が感じたことを書こう。

----

④　AI was created / after World War II / by a number of scientists, / and it has been introduced / into a variety of fields today. // Some fields are basic, / while others are more **advanced**. //

⑤　Image recognition, / such as telling apples / from oranges, / is one example. // First, / the AI needs to learn / just as we humans do. // A number of apple and orange images / are delivered / to the AI. // When the AI is given a "**viewpoint**," / such as "color," / to **distinguish** the apples / from the oranges, / then it learns / to do so / even with new **incoming** apple and orange images. // This stage of learning / is called "machine learning." // At the more advanced stage / called "deep learning," / the AI learns / to find viewpoints / by itself. // This is based on / a large amount of information / from outside. // The AI then learns / how to search for **subtle** information / about apples, / such as their size, / shape / or quality, / to separate them / without any **instruction** / from human beings. //

⑥　Deep learning / is an essential part / of AI / because it has made AI / different from a simple **automation** tool. // With deep learning, / AI can usually make the best decision, / just as we humans do / in our everyday lives. //　(198 words)

◀)) **音読しよう**　　　　　　　　　　　　　　　　　　　スピーキング・トレーナー

Practice 1　スラッシュ位置で文を区切って読んでみよう ☐
Practice 2　音の変化に注意して読んでみよう ☐
TRY!　　　2分以内に本文全体を音読しよう ☐

📖 **Reading**　本文の内容を読んで理解しよう【知識・技能】【思考力・判断力・表現力】　　共通テスト

Make the correct choice to complete each sentence or answer each question. (各4点)

1.　AI ☐ .

　　① is used in the field of image recognition

　　② was created before World War II　　③ works well only in advanced fields

　　④ was established in order to distinguish apples from oranges

2.　At the stage called "machine learning," AI is given viewpoints ☐ .

　　① automatically　　　　　　　　② by humans

　　③ through new incoming images　　④ with a machine

3.　Which of the following are true about the stage called "deep learning"? (Choose two options. The order does not matter.) ☐ · ☐

　　① At this stage, AI works well enough with the information inside it.

　　② Human beings don't help AI at all at this stage.

　　③ It is more advanced than "machine learning."

　　④ This stage is less important for making AI think like human beings.

🔊 音の変化を理解して音読することができる。
📖 AI の学習に関する英文を読んで概要や要点を捉えることができる。
🔍 文脈を理解して適切な語句を用いて英文を完成することができる。
🎧 平易な英語で話される短い英文を聞いて必要な情報を聞き取ることができる。
🗣 画像認識技術について簡単な語句を用いて説明することができる。
✍ 未来の AI 製品について簡単な語句を用いて考えを表現することができる。

als

🔍 Vocabulary & Grammar　重要表現や文法事項について理解しよう【知識】　英検® GTEC®

Make the correct choice to complete each sentence. (各 2 点)

1. The girl (　　　) to write short e-mails with a smartphone.
   ① became　　　② learned　　　③ made　　　④ turned

2. The company sends (　　　) of used clothes to foreign countries every year.
   ① a number　　② an amount　　③ the amount　　④ the number

3. Salary will be based (　　　) your experiences and educational background.
   ① by　　　　　② for　　　　　③ in　　　　　④ on

4. She's going to live by (　　　) from next spring.
   ① her　　　　　② hers　　　　③ herself　　　　④ she

5. She wouldn't have met and married him if she (　　　) studied in New York.
   ① didn't have　　② hadn't　　　③ hasn't　　　④ not having

🎧 Listening　英文を聞いて理解しよう【知識・技能】【思考力・判断力・表現力】　共通テスト　CD 77

Listen to the English and make the best choice to match the content. (4 点)

① The speaker researches AI in a company in a developing country.

② The speaker's father is a member of an AI research team at the university.

③ The speaker's father works for a company developing AI.

💬 Interaction　英文を聞いて会話を続けよう【知識・技能】【思考力・判断力・表現力】　スピーキング・トレーナー　CD 78

Listen to the English and respond to the last remark. (7 点)

［メモ　　］

アドバイス スマートフォンのアプリなどが身近で考えやすい。自信がないときは probably「おそらく」などを使うとよい。

✏️ Production（Write）　自分の考えを書いて伝えよう【思考力・判断力・表現力】

Write your answer to the following question. (7 点)

Write your ideas for a future product with AI.

アドバイス In the future school, … や，In the future AI planes, … などと場面設定をしてから書き始めるとよい。

7　After your new experience / at *Amazing Supermarket*, / a worry spreads / in your mind: / "In the future, / will AI take over jobs / from human beings?" // To answer this question, / you need to think / about what AI is better at doing / than human beings / and what you can do better / than AI. //

8　It is true / that AI is better than you / when it comes to searching / for information / from a huge amount of data / and making the best decision. // However, / you have abilities / which are unique / to human beings. // You can create new ideas, / and you can love / things and people. //

9　Artists and **inventors** are **creative**. // On this point, / AI can never **replace** them. // Doctors, / **childcare** workers / and teachers / need to feel love / toward the people / they **interact** with / in their jobs. // AI, which **lacks** this feeling, / cannot do these types / of jobs. //

10　AI has huge **potential** / to make our future brighter. // It is our responsibility / to create a good society / where human beings and AI / can go hand in hand together. // (170 words)

◀)) 音読しよう　　　　　　　　　　　　　　　　　　　　　スピーキング・トレーナー
Practice 1　スラッシュ位置で文を区切って読んでみよう☐
Practice 2　音の変化に注意して読んでみよう☐
TRY!　　　　１分40秒以内に本文全体を音読しよう☐

📖 **Reading**　本文の内容を読んで理解しよう【知識・技能】【思考力・判断力・表現力】　　　共通テスト

Make the correct choice to complete each sentence or answer each question. (各4点)

1.　What AI is better at is ☐ .
　① choosing a particular object from many　② designing buildings
　③ feeling love toward people　　　　　　 ④ replacing inventors

2.　Which of the following best express the present AI? (Choose two options. The order does not matter.) ☐ ・ ☐
　① It cannot decide the best-selling book of the month.
　② It is not good at writing a poem or a play.
　③ It is useful for taking care of patients.
　④ Much improvement is needed to play with children.

3.　To ☐ is our duty for the future.
　① have new experiences　　　　　　② make a good society with AI
　③ realize our brighter future　　　　④ replace AI with humans

● 音の変化を理解して音読することができる。　　　📖 将来の AI に関する英文を読んで概要や要点を捉えることができる。
🔎 文脈を理解して適切な語句を用いて英文を完成することができる。　🎧 平易な英語で話される短い英文を聞いて必要な情報を聞き取ることができる。
💬 AI と日常生活について簡単な語句を用いて考えを表現することができる。　✍ AI の役割について簡単な語句を用いて考えを表現することができる。

oals

🔎 Vocabulary & Grammar　重要表現や文法事項について理解しよう【知識】　英検® GTEC®

Make the correct choice to complete each sentence. (各2点)

1. His singing is so great that nobody can (　　　) him.
   ① reduce ② regret ③ repair ④ replace

2. It is important for politicians to (　　　) with local citizens.
   ① interact ② interest ③ introduce ④ invite

3. A: John needs someone's help to do this job.
   B: I think so. He (　　　) experience.
   ① builds ② lacks ③ lost ④ missed

4. Countries should work hand (　　　) hand to solve many environmental problems of the world.
   ① after ② in ③ on ④ with

5. She has two sons, (　　　) both got married last year.
   ① that ② which ③ who ④ whom

🎧 Listening　英文を聞いて理解しよう【知識・技能】【思考力・判断力・表現力】　共通テスト　CD 79

Listen to the English and make the best choice to match the content. (4点)

① The speaker doesn't have a conversation robot.

② The speaker has already used an AI conversation robot before.

③ The speaker is going to buy a conversation robot.

💬 Interaction　英文を聞いて会話を続けよう【知識・技能】【思考力・判断力・表現力】　スピーキング・トレーナー　CD 80

Listen to the English and respond to the last remark. (7点)

[メモ　　　]

　アドバイス　相手の発話を参考に，日常で AI にしてもらえたら便利だと思うことを考えよう。

✍ Production (Write)　自分の考えを書いて伝えよう【思考力・判断力・表現力】

Write your answer to the following question. (7点)

What is the role of AI in human society? Write your ideas.

　アドバイス　AI と人間がどのように調和できるか，本文を参考に考えてみよう。

You are at a special exhibition / about AI. // In front of you / there are four exhibition sections / for different fields. // You are learning / about the latest AI applications / in each field. //

Transportation //

Can you imagine / all the members / of your family / playing cards, / eating lunch, / or watching videos / while your family car drives you / to your travel goal? // No one is driving the car, / but AI is! // This is no longer a dream. // Some companies are expecting / **completely self-driving** AI cars / in the near future. //

Communication //

Perhaps you have heard such words / as "**audio** recognition" and "machine **translation**." // These technologies became possible / through deep-learning AI. // Your foreign language skills / can be supported / by these technologies / when you need to communicate / with people / in different countries, / **particularly** for such events / as business meetings or traveling abroad. //

Healthcare //

AI makes medical tools and medical care / much smarter / and more patient-**specific**. // AI collects data / from many sources / and combines it / with big data. // Doctors can use the data / to give faster and better care. // Elderly patients / at many nursing homes / don't have to go / to the hospital anymore. //

Agriculture //

Agriculture is an **industry** / where AI is used widely. // AI plays three main important roles; / operating small flying machines / to take care of farming products, / monitoring **soil** conditions, / and estimating farming environments / to decide on the best moment / for planting and **harvesting**. // (228 words)

🔊 **音読しよう**　　　　　　　　　　　　　　　　　　　スピーキング・トレーナー

Practice 1　スラッシュ位置で文を区切って読んでみよう ☐
Practice 2　音の変化に注意して読んでみよう ☐
TRY!　　　　2分20秒以内に本文全体を音読しよう ☐

📖 **Reading**　本文の内容を読んで理解しよう【知識・技能】【思考力・判断力・表現力】　　　　共通テスト

Make the correct choice to complete each sentence or answer each question. (各6点)

1. AI applications for ☐ are **not** possible at this time.

   ① a conversation with people overseas　　② full automated driving

   ③ making farming plans　　　　　　　　　④ patient health management

2. Which of the following are **not** true about AI applications? (Choose two options. The order does not matter.) ☐ · ☐

   ① AI helps doctors and nurses give faster medical care.

   ② Flying machines can free farmers from harvesting agricultural products.

   ③ We may be able to watch movies in our car while driving.

   ④ With AI, you can speak French and talk with people from France.

🔍 Vocabulary & Grammar　重要表現や文法事項について理解しよう【知識】　英検® GTEC®

Make the correct choice to complete each sentence. (各2点)

1. We don't provide any CDs to customers. Instead, we offer them (　　　) data files.
   ① audio　　　　　② media　　　　　③ radio　　　　　④ studio

2. A lot of apples were damaged by the typhoon before they were (　　　).
   ① caught　　　　② harvested　　　③ planted　　　　④ shared

3. The company (　　　) the printer with the scanner to make a new product.
   ① approached　　② combined　　　③ contacted　　　④ met

4. Shall I (　　　) you to the station? It's on my way home.
   ① drive　　　　　② hurry　　　　　③ send　　　　　④ walk

5. California is a comfortable place to live because of the climate (　　　) to the West Coast area.
   ① character　　　② especially　　③ original　　　　④ specific

6. They eat dinner every night, (　　　) TV.
   ① to watch　　　② watch　　　　③ watched　　　　④ watching

7. (　　　) nothing to do, I went to bed earlier than usual.
   ① To have　　　② Had　　　　　③ Have　　　　　④ Having

8. The theater, (　　　) I used to perform in many dramas, will close next month.
   ① that　　　　　② where　　　　③ which　　　　　④ whose

🎧 Listening　英文を聞いて理解しよう【知識・技能】【思考力・判断力・表現力】　共通テスト　CD 81

Listen to the English and make the best choice to match the content. (各4点)

1. Who developed Shakey?　[　　]
   ① A research team from the Computer History Museum.
   ② Researchers at SRI.
   ③ Students at Stanford University.
   ④ Institute in California.

2. Which is true about Shakey's appearance?　[　　]
   ① It is about 150 centimeters tall.
   ② There are more than two cameras.
   ③ There are six wheels on the bottom part.
   ④ Touch sensors are on the top part.

3. For what was the radio antenna probably used?　[　　]
   ① To communicate with another computer.
   ② To listen to people.
   ③ To play the role of a camera.　　　　④ To stop the shaking of the body.

93

Jimmy Valentine was released / from **prison**, / and it was just a week later / that a safe was broken open / in Richmond, / Indiana. // Eight hundred dollars was **stolen**. // Two weeks after that, / a safe / in Logansport / was opened, / and fifteen hundred dollars / was taken. // Everyone was shocked, / as this safe was so strong / that people thought / no one could break it open. // Then / a safe / in Jefferson City / was opened, / and five thousand dollars / was stolen. //

Ben Price was a **detective**. // He was a big man, / and famous for his skill / at solving very difficult and important cases. // So now / he began / to work on these three cases. // He was the only person / who knew / how Jimmy did his job. // People / with safes / full of money / were glad / to hear / that Ben Price was at work / trying to arrest Mr. Valentine. //

One afternoon, / Jimmy Valentine and his suitcase / arrived in a small town / named Elmore. // Jimmy, / looking like an **athletic** young man / just home from college, / walked down the street / toward the hotel. //

A young lady walked / across the street, / passed him / at the corner, / and went through a door / with a sign / "The Elmore Bank" / on it. // Jimmy Valentine looked into her eyes, / forgot at once / what he was, / and became another man. // The young lady looked back at him, / and then **lowered** her eyes / as her face became red. // Handsome young men / like Jimmy / were not often seen / in Elmore. // (241 words)

🔊 **音読しよう**　　　　　　　　　　　　　　　　　　　スピーキング・トレーナー

Practice 1　スラッシュ位置で文を区切って読んでみよう ☐
Practice 2　音声を聞きながら，音声のすぐ後を追って読んでみよう ☐
TRY!　　　2分20秒以内に本文全体を音読しよう ☐

📖 **Reading**　本文の内容を読んで理解しよう【知識・技能】【思考力・判断力・表現力】　　　共通テスト

Make the correct choice to complete each sentence or answer each question. (各6点)

1. Which of the following is **not** suggested in the first paragraph? ☐
   ① Everyone was shocked to hear that Jimmy Valentine had been released from prison.
   ② Jimmy Valentine did his jobs soon after he was released from prison.
   ③ Jimmy Valentine was a criminal who opened safes and stole money.
   ④ Jimmy Valentine was very skillful at doing his job.

2. Which of the following is **not** true about Ben Price? [　　]

　① He had solved very difficult and important cases.

　② He knew how skillful Jimmy was at doing his job.

　③ He was a famous detective.

　④ He was well-known to people who had safes full of money.

3. The expression "forgot at once what he was and became another man" in the fourth paragraph is closest in meaning to "[　　]."

　① decided to break into the Elmore Bank

　② fell in love with the young lady at first sight

　③ got so shocked that he didn't know what to say

　④ lost all the memory of the past and behaved like another man

---

🔍 **Vocabulary**　重要表現について理解しよう【知識】　　　　　　　英検 ® GTEC®

Make the correct choice to complete each sentence. (各3点)

1. We opened the cage and (　　　) the bird.

　① flied　　　　② missed　　　　③ released　　　　④ removed

2. My bicycle was (　　　) while I was in the shop.

　① carried　　　② ridden　　　　③ stolen　　　　④ taken

3. France is famous (　　　) its fine food and wine.

　① as　　　　　② by　　　　　　③ for　　　　　　④ with

4. I kicked the door and broke it (　　　).

　① on　　　　　② open　　　　　③ out　　　　　　④ over

5. The men (　　　) the ship's lifeboats into the water.

　① brought　　　② lifted　　　　③ lowered　　　　④ raised

✏ **Production (Write)**　自分の考えを書いて伝えよう【思考力・判断力・表現力】

Write your answer to the following question. (7点)

　If you had been Jimmy, what would you have done after seeing the young lady?

　アドバイス　ジミーはその女性にどんな気持ちを抱いているだろうか。自分なら次にどうするか想像してみよう。

Jimmy saw a boy / playing on the steps / of the bank / and began asking him questions / about the town. // After a time, / the young lady came out of the bank. // This time / she **pretended** / not to notice the young man / with the suitcase, / and went her way. // "Isn't that young lady Polly Simpson?" / Jimmy asked the boy. //

"No," / answered the boy. // "She's Annabel Adams. // Her father is the owner / of this bank." //

Jimmy went to the hotel. // He told the hotel clerk / that his name was Ralph D. Spencer, / and that he had come / to Elmore / to look for a place / where he could set up a shoe shop. // The clerk was so impressed / by Jimmy's clothes and **manner** / that he kindly gave him as much information / about the town / as he could. // Yes, / Elmore needed a good shoe shop. // It was a **pleasant** town / to live in, / and the people were friendly. //

"Mr. Spencer" told the hotel clerk / that he would like to stay / in the town / for a few days / and look over the situation. // Mr. Ralph D. Spencer, / Jimmy Valentine's new **identity** / ―― an identity / created by a sudden attack of love / ―― remained in Elmore / and opened a shoe shop. //

Soon / his shoe shop was doing a good business, / and he won the respect / of the community. // And more importantly, / he got to know Annabel Adams. // They fell deeply in love / and started / to plan their **wedding**. // (239 words)

🔊 音読しよう

スピーキング・トレーナー

Practice 1　スラッシュ位置で文を区切って読んでみよう ☐
Practice 2　音声を聞きながら，音声のすぐ後を追って読んでみよう ☐
TRY!　　　 2分20秒以内に本文全体を音読しよう ☐

📖 **Reading**　本文の内容を読んで理解しよう【知識・技能】【思考力・判断力・表現力】　　共通テスト

Make the correct choice to complete each sentence or answer each question. (各8点)

1.　Jimmy asked a boy questions about the town to 　　　 .

① break open the safe of the bank and steal money

② get more information about the town

③ get more information about the young lady

④ set up a shoe shop in the town

2. According to the story you read, which of the following are true? (Choose two options. The order does not matter.) ⬚ ・ ⬚

① Jimmy had come to Elmore to set up a shoe shop.

② Jimmy won not only the respect of people in Elmore but also the love of Annabel Adams.

③ Soon Jimmy's shoe shop was doing good business, but he found it hard to be accepted by the community.

④ The flame of a sudden attack of love had made Jimmy quite another man.

⑤ The hotel clerk gave Jimmy as much information as he could under the impression that Jimmy was just a rich tourist.

🔍 **Vocabulary**　重要表現について理解しよう【知識】　　　　英検 ® GTEC®

Make the correct choice to complete each sentence. (各3点)

1. She (　　　) to listen, but I knew she was thinking about something else.
   ① hesitated　　② managed　　③ pretended　　④ refused

2. They spent a (　　　) day together.
   ① considerable　　② convincing　　③ pleasant　　④ satisfaction

3. Joseph went to live in America, but his family (　　　) behind in Europe.
   ① continued　　② rejected　　③ remained　　④ stood

4. They needed the money to (　　　) up their new business.
   ① bring　　② give　　③ pick　　④ set

5. I've looked (　　　) the plans, but I haven't studied them in detail.
   ① after　　② at　　③ for　　④ over

✎ **Production (Write)**　自分の考えを書いて伝えよう【思考力・判断力・表現力】

Write your answer to the following question. (9点)

Do you think your hometown is a comfortable place to live? Why or why not?

アドバイス　自分が住んでいる地域について考えてみよう。

One day, / Jimmy wrote a letter / to one of his old friends / in Little Rock. // The letter said, / "I want / to give you my tools. // You couldn't buy them / even for a thousand dollars. // I don't need them anymore / because I finished with the old business / a year ago. // I will never touch another man's money / again." //

It was a few days / after Jimmy sent his letter / that Ben Price secretly arrived / in Elmore. // He went around the town / in his quiet way / until he found out all / he wanted to know. // From a drugstore / across the street / from Spencer's shoe shop, / he watched Ralph D. Spencer / walk by. // "You think / you're going to marry the **banker's** daughter, / don't you, / Jimmy?" / said Ben / to himself, / softly. // "Well, / I'm not so sure / about that!" //

The next morning, / Jimmy had breakfast / at the Adams home. // That day, / he was going to Little Rock / to order his wedding suit, / buy something nice / for Annabel, / and give his tools away / to his friend. //

After breakfast, / several members / of the Adams family / went to the bank together / — Mr. Adams, / Annabel, / Jimmy, / and Annabel's married sister / with her two little girls, / aged five and nine. // On the way to the bank, / they waited / outside Jimmy's shop / while he ran up to his room / and got his suitcase. // Then / they went on / to the bank. // (228 words)

🔊 **音読しよう**　　　　　　　　　　　　　　　　　　　スピーキング・トレーナー

Practice 1　スラッシュ位置で文を区切って読んでみよう ☐
Practice 2　音声を聞きながら，音声のすぐ後を追って読んでみよう ☐
TRY!　　　　2分20秒以内に本文全体を音読しよう ☐

📖 **Reading**　本文の内容を読んで理解しよう【知識・技能】【思考力・判断力・表現力】　　　共通テスト

Make the correct choice to complete each sentence or answer each question. (各6点)

1. Jimmy's letter to his old friend said that ☐.

　① he had had finished with his old job

　② he was waiting for his friend to come to Elmore

　③ he would buy his tools for a thousand dollars

　④ he would close his shoe shop and retire from the business world

2. What was Ben Price like? ☐

　① Energetic but always ready to try dangerous things.

　② Hardworking but too proud of himself.

　③ Patient and careful when making judgments.

　④ Romantic and kind to people in trouble.

3. What was in "his suitcase"? ☐

① His tools for breaking safes open.

② His wedding suit, and something nice for Annabel.

③ Letters from his old friend in Little Rock.

④ Money he had stolen from safes.

🔍 Vocabulary　重要表現について理解しよう【知識】　　　英検 Ⓡ GTEC Ⓡ

Make the correct choice to complete each sentence. (各3点)

1. They moved away; they don't live here (　　　).

① anyhow　　　② anymore　　　③ anytime　　　④ anyway

2. The post office is just (　　　) the street from the movie theater.

① across　　　② around　　　③ cross　　　④ round

3. He asked her to (　　　) him and she accepted.

① get married　　② get married with　③ marry　　④ marry with

4. In supermarkets, food companies often (　　　) away samples of their products to customers.

① carry　　　② get　　　③ give　　　④ hand

5. We visited Yokohama, and went (　　　) to Tokyo.

① at　　　② for　　　③ of　　　④ on

✍ Production (Write)　自分の考えを書いて伝えよう【思考力・判断力・表現力】

Write your answer to the following question. (7点)

Do you have something so important to you that you wouldn't sell it even if you were offered thousands of dollars?

アドバイス　いくらお金を出されても売ることのできないくらい大切なものがあるかどうか，考えてみよう。

They all went into the **banking**-room / — Jimmy, / too, / for Mr. Adams' future **son-in-law** / was welcome / anywhere. // Everyone in the bank / was glad / to see the **good-looking**, nice young man / who was going to marry Annabel. // Jimmy put down the suitcase / in the corner / of the room. //

The Elmore Bank had just put in a new safe. // It was as large as a small room / and it had a very special new kind of door / that was controlled / by a clock. // Mr. Adams was very proud of this new safe / and was showing / how to set the time / when the door should open. // The two children, / May and Agatha, / enjoyed touching all the interesting parts / of its shining heavy door. //

While these things were happening, / Ben Price quietly entered the bank / and looked inside the banking-room. // He told the bank **teller** / that he didn't want anything; / he was just waiting / for a man / he knew. //

Suddenly, / there were **screams** / from the women. // May, / the five-year-old girl, / had **firmly** closed the door / of the safe / by accident, / and Agatha was inside! // Mr. Adams tried hard / to pull open the door / for a moment, / and then cried, / "The door can't be opened! // And the clock / — I haven't started it / yet." //

"Please break it open!" / Agatha's mother cried out. //

"Quiet!" / said Mr. Adams, / raising a shaking hand. // "Everyone, / be quiet / for a moment. // Agatha!" / he called as loudly / as he could. // "Can you hear me?" // They could hear, / although not clearly, / the sound / of the child's voice. // In the **darkness** / inside the safe, / she was screaming / with **fear**. // Agatha's mother, / now getting more **desperate**, / started hitting the door / with her hands. // (277 words)

🔊 **音読しよう**
Practice 1   スラッシュ位置で文を区切って読んでみよう ☐
Practice 2   音声を聞きながら，音声のすぐ後を追って読んでみよう ☐
TRY!   2分40秒以内に本文全体を音読しよう ☐

スピーキング・トレーナー

📖 **Reading**   本文の内容を読んで理解しよう【知識・技能】【思考力・判断力・表現力】   共通テスト

Make the correct choice to answer each question. (各8点)

1. According to the story you read, which of the following are **not** true? (Choose two options. The order does not matter.) ☐ ・ ☐

   ① Ben Price was waiting for a man who could tell that "Mr. Spencer" was Jimmy Valentine.

   ② Ben Price was watching all the things which were happening in the banking-room.

   ③ Everybody in the bank knew what Mr. Adams' future son-in-law was like.

   ④ Jimmy was treated as if he were already a member of the Adams family.

   ⑤ The new safe of The Elmore Bank had a special door controlled by a clock.

◀)) シャドーイングをすることができる。　　　　　　　　　　　　　　　▯ Part 4を読んで概要や要点を捉えることができる。

🔍 文脈を理解して適切な語句を用いて英文を完成することができる。

oals　　✐ "And the clock──I haven't started it yet."と言ったときの Mr. Adams の気持ちについて表現することができる。

2. Suddenly, there were screams from the women.　What happened?　☐

　① Agatha, the nine-year-old girl, began to scream with fear.

　② Agatha was locked in the safe.

　③ May, the five-year-old girl, closed the door of the safe.

　④ Mr. Adams started the clock by accident.

🔍 **Vocabulary**　重要表現について理解しよう【知識】　　　　　　　　英検 ® GTEC®

Make the correct choice to complete each sentence. (各3点)

1. We could see the cat's eyes (　　　) in the darkness.

　① reflecting　　　② shining　　　③ streaming　　　④ swinging

2. Make sure that you put the cork back (　　　) in the bottle.

　① clearly　　　② firmly　　　③ hardly　　　④ strictly

3. I knocked the vase over (　　　) accident as I was cleaning the room.

　① by　　　② for　　　③ from　　　④ in

4. Luke thought (　　　) a moment and then said, "Would you like to come, too?"

　① at　　　② for　　　③ in　　　④ on

5. He was shaking with (　　　) after the accident.

　① ease　　　② fear　　　③ fun　　　④ regret

✐ **Production (Write)**　自分の考えを書いて伝えよう【思考力・判断力・表現力】

Write your answer to the following question. (9点)

　How do you think Mr. Adams felt when he said, "And the clock ── I haven't started it yet."

　[アドバイス]　状況を整理して，自分が Mr. Adams になったつもりで考えてみよう。

Annabel turned to Jimmy. // Her large eyes were full of pain, / but not yet **despairing**. // A woman believes / that the man / she loves / can find a way / to do anything. // "Can't you do something, / Ralph? // Try, / won't you?" // He looked at her / with a strange, soft smile / on his lips / and in his eyes. //

"Annabel," / he said, / "give me that rose / you are wearing, / will you?" //

She couldn't understand / what he meant, / but she put the rose / in his hand. // Jimmy took it / and placed it / in the pocket / of his **vest**. // Then / he threw off his coat. // With that act, / Ralph D. Spencer disappeared, / and Jimmy Valentine took his place. // "Stay away from the door, / all of you," / he ordered. //

He placed his suitcase / on the table / and opened it. // From that time on, / he didn't pay any attention / to anyone else there. // Quickly / he laid the strange shining tools / on the table. // Nobody moved / as they watched him work. // Soon / Jimmy's drill was biting **smoothly** / into the **steel** door. // In ten minutes / —— faster / than he had ever done it before / —— he opened the door. //

Agatha, / completely **exhausted** / but **unharmed**, / ran into her mother's arms. // Jimmy Valentine silently put his coat back on / and walked / toward the front door / of the bank. // As he went, / he thought / he heard a voice call, / "Ralph!" // But he never **hesitated**. // At the door, / a big man was standing / in his way. // "Hello, / Ben!" / said Jimmy. // "You're here / at last, / aren't you? // Well, / let's go. // I don't care now." //

"I'm afraid / you're mistaken, / Mr. Spencer," / said Ben Price. // "I don't believe / I **recognize** you." // Then / the big detective turned away / and walked slowly down the street. // (283 words)

🔊 **音読しよう**　　　　　　　　　　　　　　　　　　　　　　スピーキング・トレーナー

Practice 1　スラッシュ位置で文を区切って読んでみよう☐
Practice 2　音声を聞きながら，音声のすぐ後を追って読んでみよう☐
TRY!　　　2分50秒以内に本文全体を音読しよう☐

📖 **Reading**　本文の内容を読んで理解しよう【知識・技能】【思考力・判断力・表現力】　　共通テスト

Make the correct choice to complete each sentence or answer each question. (各6点)

1. When he asked Annabel for the rose she was wearing, Jimmy clearly saw in his mind that ☐ .

   ① he would be able to save Agatha
   ② he would be arrested by Ben Price
   ③ he would have to say goodbye to her
   ④ he would start a new life with her

2. When he said, "Hello, Ben!", Jimmy _____ .

① expected Ben to let him go

② expected that Ben would not recognize him

③ was ready to be arrested by Ben

④ was surprised to see Ben there

3. Which of the following is **not** true? _____

① Ben didn't recognize Jimmy.

② Ben realized why Jimmy showed what he really was.

③ Ben wanted Jimmy to live a new life with Annabel.

④ Ben watched Jimmy break the safe open.

🔍 Vocabulary　重要表現について理解しよう【知識】　　　　　英検® GTEC®

Make the correct choice to complete each sentence. (各3点)

1. He (　　　) the child down gently on her bed.
   ① laid　　　　　② lain　　　　　③ lay　　　　　④ lied

2. We had been walking over 20 miles, and we were completely (　　　).
   ① bored　　　② discouraged　　　③ exhausted　　　④ frightened

3. The boy took off his clothes and (　　　) on his pajamas.
   ① got　　　　　② put　　　　　③ took　　　　　④ turned

4. "Do you love me?" she asked. He (　　　) and then said, "I'm not sure."
   ① hesitated　　② pretended　　③ remained　　④ responded

5. The men stood (　　　) our way and would not let us enter the building.
   ① by　　　　　② in　　　　　③ on　　　　　④ out of

✏ Production (Write)　自分の考えを書いて伝えよう【思考力・判断力・表現力】

Write your answer to the following question. (7点)

If you had been Ben Price, would you have arrested Jimmy? Why or why not?

アドバイス　ベン・プライスの当初の目的をふり返り，自分だったらどうするか考えてみよう。

WPM・得点一覧表

● スピーキング・トレーナーを使って，各レッスンの本文を流暢に音読できるようにしましょう。下の計算式を使って，1分あたりに音読できた語数（words per minute）を算出してみましょう。

【本文の総語数】÷【音読にかかった時間（秒）】×60＝ [　　　] wpm

Lesson		WPM	得点
1	Part 1	/ wpm	/ 40
	Part 2	/ wpm	/ 40
	Part 3	/ wpm	/ 40
	Part 4	/ wpm	/ 40
	AP	/ wpm	/ 40
	流暢さの目安	100 wpm	/ 200

Lesson		WPM	得点
2	Part 1	/ wpm	/ 40
	Part 2	/ wpm	/ 40
	Part 3	/ wpm	/ 40
	Part 4	/ wpm	/ 40
	AP	/ wpm	/ 40
	流暢さの目安	100 wpm	/ 200

Lesson		WPM	得点
3	Part 1	/ wpm	/ 40
	Part 2	/ wpm	/ 40
	Part 3	/ wpm	/ 40
	Part 4	/ wpm	/ 40
	AP	/ wpm	/ 40
	流暢さの目安	100 wpm	/ 200

Lesson		WPM	得点
4	Part 1	/ wpm	/ 40
	Part 2	/ wpm	/ 40
	Part 3	/ wpm	/ 40
	Part 4	/ wpm	/ 40
	AP	/ wpm	/ 40
	流暢さの目安	100 wpm	/ 200

Lesson		WPM	得点
5	Part 1	/ wpm	/ 40
	Part 2	/ wpm	/ 40
	Part 3	/ wpm	/ 40
	Part 4	/ wpm	/ 40
	AP	/ wpm	/ 40
	流暢さの目安	100 wpm	/ 200

Lesson		WPM	得点
6	Part 1	/ wpm	/ 40
	Part 2	/ wpm	/ 40
	Part 3	/ wpm	/ 40
	Part 4	/ wpm	/ 40
	AP	/ wpm	/ 40
	流暢さの目安	100 wpm	/ 200

Lesson		WPM	得点
7	Part 1	/ wpm	/ 40
	Part 2	/ wpm	/ 40
	Part 3	/ wpm	/ 40
	Part 4	/ wpm	/ 40
	AP	/ wpm	/ 40
	流暢さの目安	100 wpm	/ 200

Lesson		WPM	得点
8	Part 1	/ wpm	/ 40
	Part 2	/ wpm	/ 40
	Part 3	/ wpm	/ 40
	Part 4	/ wpm	/ 40
	AP	/ wpm	/ 40
	流暢さの目安	100 wpm	/ 200

Lesson		WPM	得点
9	Part 1	/ wpm	/ 40
	Part 2	/ wpm	/ 40
	Part 3	/ wpm	/ 40
	Part 4	/ wpm	/ 40
	AP	/ wpm	/ 40
	流暢さの目安	100 wpm	/ 200

Optional		WPM	得点
	Part 1	/ wpm	/ 40
	Part 2	/ wpm	/ 40
	Part 3	/ wpm	/ 40
	Part 4	/ wpm	/ 40
	Part 5	/ wpm	/ 40
	流暢さの目安	100 wpm	/ 200